TWELFTH NIGHT

OR

WHAT YOU WILL

CAMBRIDGE
UNIVERSITY PRESS
LONDON: Fetter Lane

New York
The Macmillan Co.

Bombay, Calcutta and
Madras
Macmillan and Co., Ltd.

Toronto
The Macmillan Co. of
Canada, Ltd.

Tokyo
Maruzen-Kabushiki-Kaisha

SHAKESPEARE

TWELFTH NIGHT

OR

WHAT YOU WILL

EDITED BY

A. W. VERITY, M.A.

SOMETIME SCHOLAR OF TRINITY COLLEGE

CAMBRIDGE
AT THE UNIVERSITY PRESS
1926

First Edition   1894
Reprinted (three times) 1895
                     1900
                     1902
                     1904
                     1906
                     1908
       (twice) 1909
                     1913
                     1916
                     1919
                     1921
                     1923
                     1924
                     1926
*(With additions and corrections
from time to time)*

PRINTED IN GREAT BRITAIN

NOTE

THIS volume follows in the main the plan and style of the first of the series, containing *A Midsummer-Night's Dream*. I have, however, adopted two suggestions made with reference to its predecessor, viz., that there should be more literary criticism in the *Introduction* and less etymology in the *Glossary*. Any other hints by which the series might be improved would be welcome.

I must acknowledge the assistance of several friends and my indebtedness to previous editors.

A. W. V.

October, 1894.

CONTENTS

INTRODUCTION

I

DATES OF THE PUBLICATION AND COMPOSITION OF THE PLAY

Twelfth Night was first published, so far as we know, in 1623, in the 1st Folio[1] edition of Shakespeare's plays. There is no indication that the comedy had been previously issued in Quarto.

Published in 1623.

The probable date of the composition of *Twelfth Night* is 1601. The play does not occur in the list of Shakespeare's works given by Meres[2] in his *Palladis Tamia*, which was published in the autumn of 1598. It is mentioned in an Elizabethan *Diary* (quoted below) in February, 1602. It must therefore have been composed between the autumn of 1598 and the beginning of 1602. There are extracts in it from a song ("Farewell, dear heart," II. 3. 109) which first appeared in 1601; and a passage[3] in the third Act is thought to allude to certain restrictions on the stage ordered by the Privy Council[4] in 1600 and 1601. Many modern critics assign the composition of *Twelfth Night* to the year 1601. In style and general

Written probably in 1601.

External evidence.

Internal evidence.

---

[1] The 1st Folio was the first edition of Shakespeare's collected plays.

[2] He mentions twelve of Shakespeare's plays.

[3] "Words are very rascals *since bonds disgraced them*" (III. 1. 25). For another passage which may throw some light on the date of the play see the *Note* on III. 2. 85.

[4] By an order of the Council issued in June 1600 all the playhouses except the Globe and the Fortune were to be shut up; and even at these theatres the performances were to be limited to two a week. In the next year the Council took further steps against the stage. Dramatists might well complain that "bonds" were laid upon them. See also the note on the "new map" (1600), p. 114.

character *Twelfth Night* belongs to the group of comedies
which includes *Much Ado About Nothing*, written between
1598 and 1600, and *As You Like It*, written probably in
1599.

The Elizabethan *Diary* referred to above was that of a
barrister named John Manningham, who belonged to the
Manning- Middle Temple. His *Diary* extends, with cer-
ham's Diary. tain breaks, from January 1602 to April 1603.
The entry which helps us to determine the date of *Twelfth
Night* occurs under the date of February 2, 1602, and is as
follows:

"At our feast[1], wee had a play called Twelve Night, or
Extract re- What You Will. Much like the Comedy of
ferring to Errors, or Menechmi in Plautus; but most like
"Twelfth
Night." and neere to that in Italian called Inganni[2]. A
good practise[3] in it to make the steward beleive his lady
widowe[4] was in love with him, by counterfayting a letter
as from his lady in general termes, telling him what shee
liked best in him, and prescribing his gesture in smiling,
his apparaile, &c., and then when he came to practise,
making him believe they tooke him to be mad."

---

[1] i.e. the Candlemas feast, which formerly marked the close
of the Christmas season of rejoicing. The play would be acted
in the Hall of the Middle Temple (cf. 1 *Henry VI*, II. 4. 3). The
Christmas-tide festivities, called "Revels" (see G.), of the four
Legal Societies (Inner Temple, Middle Temple, Gray's Inn,
and Lincoln's Inn) were conducted on a great scale, and always
included the acting of plays. These Societies were specially
noted for their costly Masques; see the Essay on the Masque
prefixed to Milton's *Comus*, Pitt Press edition.

[2] Really *Twelfth Night*, as we shall see, resembles the Italian
play *Ingannati* more than that "called *Inganni*."

[3] i.e. trick, scheme; cf. v. 360.

[4] "It is possible that in the form in which the comedy was
performed on Feb. 2, 1602, she was a widow, and that the author
subsequently made the change; but it is more likely, as Olivia
must have been in mourning for the loss of her brother, that
Manningham mistook her condition, and concluded hastily that
she lamented the loss of her husband."—Collier.

II

THE TITLE OF THE PLAY

January 6, the festival of the Epiphany and the *twelfth day* from Christmas, was formerly kept with numerous ceremonies and festivities[1]. A common feature of these festivities at Court and at the houses of great nobles was the performance of plays. No doubt, *Twelfth Night* was so called because it was written for performance on Twelfth-Night—possibly at Court[2]—and embodied the genial spirit of the Twelfth-Night festivities and revels. In the same way, *A Midsummer-Night's Dream* owed its title to the fact that it was designed for representation on Midsummer-Night and embodied the traditional associations of Midsummer-Night. Each play took its name from a festival. Each harmonised with the traditions of the festival.

The Twelfth-Night festival in Shakespeare's time.

Celebrated with plays.

This play written for Twelfth-Night: hence its title.

Compare "A Midsummer-Night's Dream."

The secondary title *What You Will* seems to refer to the character of the piece. It is a combination of comedy and romance, touched in the love-scenes with a sentiment that becomes serious, if not tragic. Shakespeare seems to forestall the objection that the play belongs to no particular type of drama, and is hard to describe, by saying—'call it comedy or romance, *What You Will*.' Compare the similar title of the similar work *As You Like It*. Some, however, think that he meant: 'if you do not approve of the title *Twelfth Night*, then call it what you will, by any title you please.'

Its second title: "What You Will."

[1] See the account in Brand's *Popular Antiquities*.

[2] It has been conjectured that *Twelfth Night* was one of four plays the performance of which before Queen Elizabeth in the Christmas season of 1601–2 is recorded, though their names are not.

III

THE "SCENE" OF THE PLAY'S ACTION

The locality of the events of *Twelfth Night* is not shown by any stage-direction in the 1st Folio. It is indicated, however, by allusions such as "This is Illyria, lady" (1. 2. 2). Most modern texts describe the "Scene" as "A city in Illyria, and the sea-coast near it."

We may identify "Illyria[1]" (so far as we regard it as a definite region) with the modern Dalmatia[2], on the east coast of the Adriatic. From its association with Venice this country was probably regarded as more or less Italian[3] by the Elizabethans. Shakespeare, however, does not really connect the events of *Twelfth Night* with any precise locality; the play has no touches descriptive of the country such as occur in *The Merchant of Venice*[4]. Its "Illyria" is no less imaginary and indefinite a realm than the "Bohemia" of *The Winter's Tale*; and the vagueness is appropriate to a romance. Equally indefinite, of course, is the period in which the events are supposed to happen.

The country of "Illyria."

IV

THE PROBABLE SOURCES OF CERTAIN ELEMENTS OF THE PLAY

Many of Shakespeare's plots are not original. He often takes some existing story and re-tells it, re-creating the characters in it and adding new ones, with new incidents. He has done this in the case of *Twelfth Night*.

[1] The ordinary Greek name was Ἰλλυρίς—the Latin, *Illyricum*.
[2] Its chief city in Shakespeare's time was Spalatro, famous for the ruins of Diocletian's palace; I cannot help wondering whether he had them in mind when he made Antonio speak of
"the memorials and the things of fame
That do renown this city" (III. 3. 23, 24).
[3] Cf. the Italian names in the play.
[4] Cf. the allusions to the "Rialto" (I. 3. 20, 39, 50), and the "tranect" (III. 4. 53).

The play falls into two divisions: plot (serious) and underplot (comic).

The plot or serious element is the love-story in which Olivia, Viola, Orsino and Sebastian figure. *The plot or serious ele- ment of the play.* Closely connected with the love-story towards the close of the play is the confusion produced by the resemblance between Viola and Sebastian.

The underplot or comic element is the intrigue against Malvolio. Of course, the two elements, the *The underplot or comic ele- ment.* serious and the comic, are so blended[1] that a division of this kind cannot be quite satis- factory. Plot and underplot are carefully made to overlap. Still, the division seems to give a fairly correct *Union of plot and underplot.* notion of the substance of the play.

Of the underplot we may say at once that it is all, so far as is known, of Shakespeare's own in- *The underplot original.* vention[2].

With the plot the case stands otherwise; as Grant White says:

"The story of a woman serving her lover in the disguise of a page, and pleading his cause with her rival, *The plot not original.* who falls in love with her, seems to have been considered common property by the novelists[3] and play- wrights of the 16th century."

Similarly, the confusions arising through the likeness of two members of a family might also be described as "the common property" of playwrights and novelists[4]. We find

[1] Note, for example, how the incident of the duel (III. 4), and the encounters which arise through it (IV. 1 and V. 175–215), unite the plot and underplot by bringing together the characters of each: Viola, Olivia and Sebastian on the one hand—Sir Toby, Sir Andrew and Fabian on the other.

[2] Shakespeare's underplots are usually original.

[3] The story is told, with variations, in three well-known col- lections of tales: in Bandello's *Novelle* (1554); in Cinthio's *Hecatomithi* (1565); and in Belleforest's French *Histoires Tragiques*, where it is adapted from the Italian of Bandello.

[4] This idea is the basis of *The Comedy of Errors* and of the *Menaechmi* of Plautus on which *The Comedy of Errors* was founded; and Manningham was reminded of both these plays when he saw *Twelfth Night*. Plautus took the notion from the

this notion combined with the above-mentioned story in
a novel which was undoubtedly the main source
The main Source used by Shakespeare. of the plot of *Twelfth Night*. This novel was
Barnabe Rich's *Historie of Apolonius and Silla*,
one of a collection of eight tales called *Riche His Farewell to
the Militarie Profession* (1581), taken from foreign sources.

Viola's resemblance to Sebastian; her resolve to serve
Orsino disguised as a page and then falling in love with
him; her involuntarily winning Olivia's love while she
pleads Orsino's cause; Olivia's espousal of Sebastian in
mistake for Cesario (Viola), and Orsino's transferring his
love from Olivia to Viola: all these details and incidents
find their counterpart in Rich's novel. Shakespeare re-told
the story, refining it and making it far more effective for
dramatic purposes.

Practically the same story forms the subject of an anony-
Another pro- bable Source. mous Italian play called *Gl' Ingannati*[1], 'The
Cheated,' which was acted at Siena in 1531
and printed at Venice in 1537. In all essentials the plot of
the *Ingannati* presents a close resemblance to the plot of
The signifi- cant name "Malevolti." *Twelfth Night*; and in its introduction (*Il
Sacrificio*) occurs the name *Malevolti*, which
is certainly suggestive of Shakespeare's *Mal-
volio*, while one of the characters in the play itself bears the
name *Fabio*, which recalls Olivia's servant *Fabian*. That the
Ingannati was known to Shakespeare seems certain.

One other work must be mentioned. This also is an
A third Source. Italian play, with a title similar to that of the
last mentioned. It is a piece named *Gl' In-
ganni*, 'The Cheats' (1592), written by a certain Curzio
Gonzaga. The *Inganni* does not bear so striking a resem-

Greek stage. "Greek comedies turning on the likeness of twins
seem to have been invariably called Δίδυμοι, and plays under
this title are mentioned from the hands of six different authors,"
A. W. Ward, *Dramatic Literature*, I. 374. Gk. δίδυμος = 'twin.'

[1] The Prologue of the *Ingannati* expressly claims that the story
is original—"never before seen nor read." Perhaps therefore
the *Ingannati* furnished Bandello and Cinthio with the story as
told in their collections of tales. The history of any widely spread
story or legend is always difficult (if not impossible) to trace.

blance as the *Ingannati* to *Twelfth Night*, but it is noticeable
for this reason: the sister who disguises herself *The name*
in male attire (and is thereby mistaken for her *"Cesare."*
brother whom she resembles) assumes the name *Cesare*,
and *Cesare* is almost as suggestive of *Cesario* as *Malevolti*
of *Malvolio*.

How, it may be asked, could these Italian plays be known
to Shakespeare? I think it very probable that *Shakespeare*
Shakespeare was sufficiently a master of Italian *and Italian*
to be able to read the plays in the original; and *literature.*
we know that a great quantity of Italian literature came
into England. English translations too of
Italian works were very numerous; there may *Many Italian*
have been Elizabethan versions or adaptations, *works trans-*
now lost, of the *Ingannati* and Gonzaga's *In-* *lish.* *lated into Eng-*
ganni. There was certainly a French translation of the
Ingannati under the title *Les Abusés*; and we may credit
Shakespeare with a tolerable knowledge of French, if not
of Italian. Moreover, "an Italian troupe of players visited
England in 1577–78 and played before the Queen at Windsor, and may have had the play, which was very popular
in Italy, with them." The fact that Manningham noticed
the resemblance suggests that one of these Italian comedies
was familiar, somehow, to Elizabethan playgoers.

I should say, then, with regard to the sources of the plot
of *Twelfth Night* that the three works which claim chief
attention as having furnished Shakespeare with some
materials for his play are:

(1) Rich's *Historie of Apolonius and Silla* (1581), un-
questionably the most important source[1];

[1] As Rich's tale (1) contained the essential elements of the
plot of *Twelfth Night* and (2) was in English, there is no need to
suppose that Shakespeare consulted foreign sources such as
Bandello and Cinthio and Belleforest, whose collections of stories
(*Novelle* or *Histoires*) are associated with other plays of Shakespeare.

The names *Malevolti* and *Cesare constitute the indication* that
Shakespeare knew the two Italian comedies, to which Manning-
ham's remark drew attention. The mixture of foreign and
English names of characters is, of course, quite Elizabethan.

Benvolio is a minor character in *Romeo and Juliet*.

(2) the anonymous Italian comedy *Gl' Ingannati* (1531);

(3) Gonzaga's play *Gl' Inganni* (1592).

It must not be supposed that Shakespeare's indebtedness to these sources amounts to much. The poetry of *Twelfth Night*; its romance and humour; the manner in which

The extent of Shakespeare's indebtedness.

ideas borrowed from other writers are turned to finer issues and improved upon; the whole of the comic underplot; the skilful interweaving of the comic and serious parts; above all, the characterisation: these things, which make *Twelfth Night* the beautiful work it is, are absolutely Shakespeare's own.

V

SOME CHARACTERISTICS OF THE PLAY

Twelfth Night has always been a favourite play with students of Shakespeare. Its charm lies primarily in the union of humour with romance, of diverting action with masterly characterisation.

There is the obvious humour of the scenes in which

Humour.

Malvolio is tricked; of the revelling-scenes wherein Sir Andrew is made the butt of his wittier companions; of the duel-scene; and of the confusions that arise through the resemblance of the brother and sister. And a less obvious but equally delightful humour animates many another incident and idea in the play. Thus Orsino's protesting a changeless love for Olivia —and transferring that love to Viola (with Olivia's full approbation); Olivia's protesting that for seven summers she will keep fresh a "brother's dead love" in cloistered seclusion from the sight of men—and falling in love with the first handsome young man who crosses her path (we hear no more of the dead brother); the fatuous Sir Andrew's presumption in paying court to the rather imperious Countess; Sebastian's calm acceptance of Olivia for a wife, and easy self-confidence in his love-affairs, so unlike the tortures of anxiety endured by Olivia and Viola and Orsino: all these things surely (and much else) were "intimated" to the poet by the very "spirit of humours."

The humour of *Twelfth Night* is certainly one of its chief charms.

Its effect is set off and heightened by combination with a romantic strain. "Romantic" as applied to incident suggests something remote from actual *Romance.* experience, lying beyond the scope of everyday life. The tone of *Twelfth Night* is in this sense romantic. Some of the incidents which we have just cited as illustrations of Shakespeare's humour have also an element of romance; and the play as a whole is romantic in that it is made up of events which, being individually out of the common, assume a tinge of improbability when brought together. Not that this improbability (perhaps I should say un-reality) strikes us as we read[1] the play, because we feel, or ought to feel, from the outset that we are moving in a world of romance and whimsical intrigue in which the prosaic conditions of real life and its sober tests do not apply.

Considered merely as a tale *Twelfth Night* is interesting. There are comedies in which the interest turns more on the characters than on the action. But in *Action.* *Twelfth Night* the story itself interests and diverts. Our attention is held by what happens.

Of the characters something will be said later. Charac-terisation is the great feature of Shakespeare's *Characterisa-* plays, and the characterisation of *Twelfth* *tion.* *Night* is no exception.

Another notable quality of this play is its harmony of design and execution. It is a complete and *Harmonious* uniform work: "appearing to have been struck *style, uniform-* *ity, and com-* out at a heat, as if the whole plot, its characters *pleteness.* and dialogue, had presented themselves at once, in one

---

[1] The case is perhaps different when we see the play acted, and *Twelfth Night* does not for stage-purposes rank among quite the best of Shakespeare's comedies. Thus its stage-history will not bear comparison with that of *Much Ado About Nothing*. The reason, I think, is that in actual representation the unreality of a romance becomes too apparent. Romantic incidents, to be effective, should be imagined, not seen. These remarks would also apply to *A Midsummer-Night's Dream*, a piece that is comparatively seldom revived on the London stage nowadays.

harmonious group, before the 'mind's eye' of the poet, previously to his actually commencing the formal business of writing[1]."

Thus the plot and underplot are worked out, with no omissions or superfluous details, so that each part is fitted to its place; and they are combined into a harmonious whole.

In some plays the interest flags at times; or the work does not keep at the same level. *Twelfth Night* is not marred by inequalities; there are no ups and downs. Its characteristic is an even, sustained excellence.

Again, the action, characterisation, and diction of the play are suited to each other. There is no elaborate or subtle character-drawing, except possibly in the case of Malvolio. The *dramatis personæ* are depicted with few but vivid strokes: a method which fits the rapid movement of the play, for amid busy intrigues and a succession of amusing incidents there is no place for complex studies of human nature. And as the characterisation is adapted to the action, so is the diction appropriate to both—light and pointed in the colloquial, comic scenes of the underplot, but informed in the serious parts with a poetic grace finely expressive of the comedy's higher strain of romance and sentiment. Justly then do critics dwell on the "perfect unity" of *Twelfth Night*.

Another feature is the genial spirit that pervades the piece—its tone of pure kindliness and pleasure.

Genial spirit.

"This," says Hazlitt[2], "is justly considered as one of the most delightful of Shakespear's comedies. It is full of sweetness and pleasantry. It is perhaps too good-natured for comedy. It has little satire, and no spleen. It aims at the ludicrous rather than the ridiculous. It makes us laugh at the follies of mankind, not despise them, and still less bear any ill-will towards them." We cannot help thinking that *Twelfth Night* was the outcome of a period of serenity; though it has the necessary hints at life's shadows.

[1] Verplanck.   [2] *Characters of Shakespear's Plays*.

VI

THE CHARACTERS OF THE PLAY

The heroine is Viola, since her assumption of disguise is the motive-spring of the plot, and our sympathies are mainly centred upon her. To think of *Twelfth Night* is to think at once of Viola.

Viola.

She is characterised by the essentially feminine qualities of tenderness, modesty and shrinking delicacy of feeling. These qualities become more conspicuous when we compare her with other maidens in Shakespeare who assume the disguise of male attire. Rosalind for instance has a buoyant vitality of spirit that carries her through difficulties; Portia can trust in any emergency to her virile intellect, ready wit and force of will. Viola does not possess these gifts; she is a graceful, imaginative girl who has conceived a plan that brings her into hazardous places through which she has scarce strength of heart or head to steer her course. She is filled with "a sweet consciousness of her feminine nature," and though she plays her part creditably, "never forgets, nor allows us to forget, that she is playing a part[1]."

Her girlishness reveals itself in little ways; and when she is confronted with danger, as in the duel-scene, she almost breaks down in her disguise, and we wonder whether the discovery can be delayed. This antithesis between the boldness of her scheme, with its attendant pretence of manhood[2], and the girlish gentleness of her nature has a great charm and humour.

Viola is very loyal and true. Herself in love with Orsino, she still pleads for him most earnestly with Olivia—indeed, with far greater earnestness than he had manifested in his own suit. She would never dream of playing him false:

"I'll do my best
To woo your lady—[*Aside*] Yet, a barful strife!
Whoe'er I woo, myself would be his wife."

[1] Mrs Jameson, *Characteristics of Women*.
[2] A pretty comic touch is her use of bold slang phrases like "Westward-ho!" (said with a fine assumption of mannishness), III. I. 145.

Her love, quiet and unchanging, contrasts with Orsino's fickle, over-eloquent fancy, no less than with Olivia's impetuous passion. And it is marked by a lowliness very characteristic of her modest nature; for she seems quite content to accept Orsino's love at second-hand. Would Portia or Rosalind have been so acquiescent?

Olivia is a great lady, dignified and competent. She rules

Olivia. her household and directs its affairs with ease and discretion, as Sebastian notices directly. The members of the household evidently stand in awe of their mistress. That she has admirable common sense may be inferred from her remarks about the Clown and her reproof to Malvolio (1. 5. 97–104).

She is somewhat cold and self-contained; inclined to keep her social inferiors at a distance. Thus there is no familiarity between her and her gentlewoman Maria. "I see you what you are, you are too proud," says Viola at their first meeting. It may be partly the pride of rank: it is doomed to be humbled.

For by a freak of fortune Olivia falls suddenly and completely in love with the Duke's page, though she will have none of the Duke himself.

No longer reserved, no longer careful about her rank, she deigns to woo him, and his opposition only increases her wilful determination, since she is so accustomed to have her own way. She knows of course that she is giving cause for unfriendly criticism of her conduct, the more so because she had protested her intention to withdraw from the world; yet she pursues her object persistently, and ends by throwing all dignity and decorum to the winds and carrying her lover (as she supposes) off to the church.

As with Viola, there is an antithesis between the natural character of Olivia and the part which a caprice of fortune leads her to play. Stated barely, her conduct appears somewhat indelicate; yet no such impression occurs to us in reading the piece because the whole story is treated in a spirit of pure romance. It is all too fanciful and poetic to be taken and criticised very seriously. Compared with Viola, Olivia does not appeal very strongly to our sympathies, though there is a strain of kindliness in her[1].

It is as Malvolio's foe that Maria, the sharp and witty of tongue, is prominent. She originates the plot against him, carries it through, and when it is reaching its end passes out of the play. In her scheming against Malvolio she seems to be the very spirit of malicious wit assailing its natural enemy, solemn dulness. She is typically appropriate to a comedy of intrigue, and moves in it as in her element. Intrigue is needed to bring out the points of such a character.

Maria.

Maria has wonderful sharpness of insight as of speech. She reads Malvolio's character through and through, and perceives defects hidden from all the others (except perhaps the Clown). Hence in her letter she is able to play precisely upon his weaknesses and advise him to commit the very faults to which he is prone; and when he comes into Olivia's presence with his loverlike airs how adroitly does her question "Why appear you?" (III. 4. 40, 41) lead him on to cut the most ridiculous figure.

Another proof of her cleverness is the ease with which she adapts herself to those about her: merry enough with Sir Toby and his friends, but demure before Olivia. She has ambition; she means all along to marry Sir Toby and become "my lady." Her design is no secret; the Clown jokes her about it (I. 5. 29), and Sir Toby is complacently conscious that she "adores" him (II. 3. 196). Probably it is as much with a view to pleasing Sir Toby (who cannot endure Malvolio) as to gratifying her own dislike of the steward that she proposes, and takes so much pains to carry out, the plot. Its success at any rate leads to the much desired result, Sir Toby marrying her "in recompense" (V. 372) of her cleverness and trouble[2].

[1] Cf. her anxiety about Malvolio (III. 4. 67–70), and her pity for him in his humiliation (V. 353–363, 377).

[2] Cf. his remark "I could marry this wench for this device," said at the end of the letter-scene, II. 5. 200.

Orsino[1] is an attractive figure:

Orsino. "Of fresh and stainless youth;
In voices well divulg'd, free, learn'd, and valiant,
And in dimension and the shape of nature
A gracious person."

He is kindly and courteous to all; eloquent and full of
poetic thoughts and sentiment. Yet, though he may win
sympathy at first he does not retain it; we begin after a
time to doubt the genuineness of his feeling. It is a self-
conscious melancholy in which really he delights. He feeds
on his love as on some dainty fare. He makes it serve as an
occasion of fine speeches; for, like Shakespeare's Richard II,
he is a *connoisseur* of phrases. As he speaks of his sorrows
he is not the true lover but the literary artist using his own
emotions as a "subject." Like Richard, he *does* little: he
merely talks most beautifully and pays court by deputy
instead of going himself. When at the close he calmly
transfers to Viola what he supposes to be his affections we
are not surprised: we have ceased to believe much in them.
His love of Olivia was almost a fiction; she had only "enchanted his imagination, not won his heart," just as Othello
fascinated the girlish fancy of Desdemona rather than really
won her love. We may doubt indeed whether Orsino would
ever be much in love with anyone but himself. An amiable
egoist, he would always remain in his own eyes the person
of chief consequence, and accept Viola's devotion as a
matter of course.

Malvolio has much to recommend him[2]. He seems a
capable and trustworthy man, sober and diligent
Malvolio. in discharge of duties. Olivia turns to him in any
difficulty, evidently relying on his discretion (I. 5. 116,
318, II. 3. 77, III. 4. 5–7). She is much concerned about
his supposed malady, and "would not have him miscarry
for the half of her dowry" (III. 4. 67–70). Her good
opinion is strong testimony to his merits. Unfortunately

---

[1] The name, no doubt, was suggested by that of the great
Italian family of *Orsini*. He is described as a Duke only in the
first Act; in the rest of the play he is called 'Count.'

[2] It was Charles Lamb's view that Malvolio "is not essentially
ludicrous," but "becomes comic by accident."

those merits are marred by a defect which Olivia describes
with precision when she says, "O you are sick of self-love,
Malvolio" (I. 5. 97).

"Self-love" implies extreme self-conceit and vanity.
With Malvolio "self-love" is what Pope calls "the ruling
passion." It dominates his whole character. Self-conceited people of a serious turn are apt to be censorious and
find fault; they judge others by the lofty standard of their
own imaginary excellencies and find them wanting. Malvolio has a positive gift for fault-finding. With what
unctuous satisfaction does he deliver Olivia's reprimand
to the revellers and reprove Maria (II. 3. 93–109, 130–133)!
How he enjoys the thought of censuring Sir Toby and
bidding him "amend his ways" (II. 5. 61–81)! His bearing
towards his fellow-servants may be inferred from Maria's
remark that if he does go mad, and has to be confined, "the
house will be the quieter" (III. 4. 147). Even in such a
small matter as overtaking Viola and giving her Olivia's
ring he lets his weakness steal out: "You might have saved
me my pains" (II. 2. 5, 6). Malvolio in short is one of those
over-virtuous people who love virtue not only—perhaps,
not chiefly—for its own sake but for the right that it gives
them (they suppose) to judge and condemn their neigh-
bours.

He has not a grain of humour—indeed, self-conceit and
humour are incompatible—and little sympathy with his
fellow-creatures: the self-conceited are too much wrapt
up in themselves to have wide views and tastes. Hence
Malvolio takes things too seriously[1] and regards all that
lies outside his own narrow sympathies as wrong. Dis-
inclined to carouse, he thinks indulgence in "cakes and ale"
an unpardonable "disorder." Too dull to see a joke, he
looks on the Clown's jests as offences against sense (I. 5.
89–96). Such men magnify trifles into grave misdemeanours.

His vanity about his personal appearance and manners is
ludicrous. He "practises behaviour"; is confident that his
"complexion," if any, will touch Olivia, and that all who
look on him *must* love him; is not unconcerned about his

---

[1] He mistakes "bird-bolts" for "cannon-bullets" (I. 5. 100).

dress—"branched velvet gowns" and the like; and feels
that a grand air, "the humour of state," will become him
mightily.

He has an overweening sense of his own importance, and
forgets that he is not "any more than a steward" (II. 3.
123). The other members of the household are in his eyes
"lighter people," "idle shallow things," whose element he
is above (III. 4. 136, 137).

In fact, Malvolio has the most exalted opinion of his own
merits: is "the best persuaded of himself,...*crammed*, as
he thinks, with excellencies[1]" (II. 3. 162, 163); and the
signal proof of his mingled self-conceit, want of humour,
personal vanity and self-importance is the readiness where-
with he credits the preposterous idea that Olivia loves him
—and "stoops to conquer." That she, graced with youth
and beauty, rank and wealth, and wooed by the charming
Orsino, sovereign of the realm, should prefer her prosaic
house-steward: this notion does not strike Malvolio as at
all strange—"there is example for 't," he reflects: and
what[2] more can be said?

Yet one is a little sorry for him. He suffers, surely, more
than he deserves, and the scene of the "dark room" (IV. 2)
has pathos as well as humour. The bitterness of the humiliation inflicted upon Malvolio almost raises it into the region
of tragedy, for mortifying as it would be to any one, it must
be well-nigh intolerable to a man of his temperament.
Olivia's sympathy, however, may be some salve to his
wounded *amour propre* (V. 353–363, 377).

Sir Toby, with his wit, relish of humour and genius
for sociability, reminds us in a far-off way of
Falstaff, and inspires something of the liking
which we cannot help feeling for his greater prototype.
Perhaps we ought not to like this rollicking toper any more

Sir Toby.

---

[1] Note specially the whole of Maria's description of him (II. 3).
[2] Maria hints at another aspect of his character when she
speaks of him as a "time-pleaser" (II. 3. 160). We may well
attribute to his censoriousness a touch of that hypocrisy from
which the Puritanism of some was not exempt. A conscientious
Puritan would not have followed the injunction about the
"yellow stockings"; and then that "branched velvet gown"!

than Sir John, but most of us do, in an apologetic fashion:
he has such a genial way with him, so keen a sense of fun,
such good temper. He is brave too (unlike Sir Andrew)
and manly: witness his readiness in encountering Sebastian.
He treats his friend shabbily, fooling money out of him,
but does it with a diverting adroitness which makes the
jest of the whole business hide the meanness of his conduct.
For all his intercourse with the servants of the household,
he retains a sense of his rank, and it comes out very comic-
ally at times, as in the letter-scene when Malvolio presumes
to call him "kinsman" (II. 5. 61). He has a rough and ready
sort of cleverness that gratifies his love of fun by devising
comic situations such as the episode of the duel (where he
shows skill in bringing the unwilling combatants together).
But his cleverness is outdone by Maria's: admiration of her
scheme brings matters to a crisis between them; and by a
fine turn of poetic justice, while he is ridiculing Malvolio
for falling an easy victim to the trick, he is himself caught
in her net. And, if we mistake not, she will keep him in
better order with that sharp tongue.

Sir Andrew is the butt on whom Sir Toby (like Maria
and the Clown) exercises his wit: foolish himself, he is the cause of admirable fooling in *Sir Andrew.*
others. He is also the echo[1] of his friend in such kind that
apart from his dulness he can scarcely be said to have any
personality. He follows Sir Toby's lead always; repeats his
"very phrases"; and whatever Sir Toby bids him do,
whether it be to stay a week longer or write a challenge,
mildly acquiesces. Up to the very end no suspicion of his
friend's false play crosses his thoughts. His confidence and
admiration remain unshaken (V. 196–198); and his last
words in the play are an offer of assistance to Sir Toby so
that they may keep "together" (V. 210, 211). Sir Andrew
typifies the fantastic fool—Malvolio, the solemn coxcomb;
but whereas Malvolio perceives how he has been treated
and thus stirs our sympathy, Sir Andrew is armed with the

---

[1] See I. 3. 67, 68, note; and cf. *The Merry Wives of Windsor*,
where Slender is the "echo" of Justice Shallow. This feature
of Sir Andrew's character is *much emphasised* in the play.

happy unconsciousness and self-content of true imbecility, so that pity were merely wasted upon him. His cowardice needs no comment.

The Clown Feste[1] shows himself a shrewd observer of
The Clown. men and things; he judges Orsino aright (II. 4. 75–81), and perhaps Malvolio too (I. 5. 84–87). His insight into character is combined with versatility; he readily estimates the company in which he is and suits his bearing to it, always "adapting himself to the mood of the moment[2]." Thus, he humours the sentimental Duke by singing him dreamy, old-world ballads; yet joins the two knights in their carouse, talks amusing nonsense, and starts the "catch." To quote his own description of himself, he is "for all waters" (i.e. ready to play whatever part the occasion requires), and fulfils Viola's estimate (III. 1. 67–74) of the complete jester, observing the "mood" and "quality" of those on whom he jests, and "the time." Indirectly his songs, in their varied style, illustrate the different characters of the people to whom they are addressed, and thus have a dramatic relation to the general movement of the piece.

He is less wise and "deep-contemplative[3]" than Touchstone in *As You Like It* (with whom one naturally compares him). Touchstone, having seen "cities of men and manners," is more of a philosopher, and more of a satirist; a jaded courtier, he uses his folly as a cloak for railing sarcasm against the world and its ways; there is method —and bitterness—in his madness. Feste inclines rather to the cap-and-bells side of his profession. A practical joke like the part he plays in the "dark room" suits him, but would scarcely suit Touchstone. Feste is rather the jester; better tempered, if less pointed, in his folly. He has more humour; Touchstone more wit. Yet his cleverness is such that only by irony is he called "the Fool" of the play; for

[1] From Lat. *festus*, 'cheerful, gay'; a fitting name for a jester.
[2] Gervinus, who brings out this point admirably.
[3] Cf. *As You Like It*, II. 7. 30–32:

"My lungs began to crow like chanticleer,
    That *fools* should be so *deep-contemplative*,
    And I did laugh."

those who are really made to appear as fools are Sir Andrew, a "natural," and Malvolio, a "wise man folly-fallen."

We see little of Sebastian, but that little leaves a pleasant impression. Perhaps the most striking feature of his character, and dramatically the most *Sebastian.* important because of the contrast which it points, is his blunt, downright simplicity, which finds vent in vigorous deeds. Unlike Orsino, he acts, and neither reflects nor talks much. Picture Orsino in his place when Olivia mistakes him for Cesario: how subtly Orsino would have analysed the situation, how eloquent and poetical he would have been, and how irresolute! Sebastian merely offers some commonplace remarks on the strangeness of the affair, quickly grasps the essential facts that Olivia is a desirable wife and wants to marry him, and makes no more ado about settling the matter straightway than about repaying Sir Andrew's rash blows. This plain practicality stands out effectively in a piece so full of sentiment; and his entire naturalness is a relief after the artificial self-consciousness of Olivia and Orsino.

VII

OUTLINE OF THE STORY OF THE PLAY

Act I., Scene 1. At the palace of Orsino, Duke of Illyria. We hear of his suit to the Countess Olivia, who rejects his offers of love.

Scene 2. On the coast of Illyria. Viola, a young girl of noble birth, has just been wrecked with her twin-brother, Sebastian; she does not know whether or not he has been lost in the wreck. Learning from the captain of the ship-wrecked vessel that the ruler of the country is Duke Orsino, a former friend of her dead father, she conceives the plan of disguising herself as a page-boy and entering Orsino's service.

Scene 3. At the house of Olivia. The scene introduces us to three characters who will be conspicuous in the under-plot, viz. Olivia's maid, Maria; her kinsman, Sir Toby Belch; and his friend, Sir Andrew Aguecheek, a foolish knight, who, at Sir Toby's instigation, is a suitor for Olivia's hand.

Scene 4. At Orsino's palace. Viola has carried out her plan, and is now, under the name Cesario, a page of Orsino. She is sent by Orsino to plead his cause with Olivia. *Viola herself has fallen in love with Orsino.*

Scene 5. At Olivia's house. We meet three new characters—Olivia; the Clown, Feste, the jester of her household; and the prim, rather puritanical, steward, Malvolio. Orsino's messenger, Cesario (Viola), arrives, is admitted to Olivia's presence, and pleads for Orsino. *Olivia falls in love with Cesario,* whom she believes, of course, to be a young man. Cesario leaves, and Olivia sends a ring after him, and bids him come again.

(The position therefore of the love-affairs at the end of the first Act is this: Orsino loves Olivia; Viola loves Orsino; Olivia loves Viola, i.e. Cesario.)

Act II., Scene 1. On the coast of Illyria. Sebastian, Viola's twin-brother, was saved at the wreck by a sailor, Antonio. He is now telling Antonio about his sister, Viola —*how much she resembled him.* He believes that she has perished. Bidding farewell to Antonio, he goes on his way to Orsino's court. Antonio, who has conceived a strong liking for Sebastian, follows him.

Scene 2. Near Olivia's house. Malvolio overtakes Viola (Cesario), who has just left Olivia, and gives her the ring sent by Olivia. Viola guesses the secret of Olivia's love.

Scene 3. At Olivia's house: a revelling scene. Sir Toby, Sir Andrew, and the Clown are drinking and singing. Maria comes to tell them that Olivia is vexed at the disturbance. Then Malvolio enters and reprimands them in Olivia's name. On his departure Maria proposes a scheme against him: she will compose a letter which shall delude him into believing that his mistress, Olivia, is in love with him.

Scene 4. At Orsino's palace: a scene of sentiment, in which the chief actors are Orsino and Viola, who speaks the famous lines " She never told her love." Orsino again sends Viola to Olivia. (The interest of the scene lies in the fuller revelation of Orsino's character and of Viola's feelings towards him.)

Scene 5. In Olivia's garden. Malvolio finds the letter written by Maria and is deluded exactly as she wished.

Act III., Scene 1. In Olivia's garden. Viola enters, and meets the Clown; he goes into the house to tell Olivia of Viola's coming. The rest of the scene passes between Viola and Olivia who reveals her love of the page. Viola repels Olivia's overtures.

Scene 2. At Olivia's house. Sir Andrew has seen the meeting of Olivia and Viola in the last scene, and is jealous of the favour shown by the Countess to the page. Sir Toby, knowing Sir Andrew to be a coward, persuades him to challenge Viola to a duel.

Scene 3. A street in the city. Sebastian and Antonio have arrived in the town, though Antonio knows that for certain reasons it is dangerous for him to be there. Antonio lends Sebastian his purse and goes off to seek a lodging, while Sebastian wanders about the town. (Sebastian and Viola being in the same city, and Viola being dressed as a young man—indeed, like her brother, III. 5. 416–418, v. 241—we now expect confusions to arise from the resemblance between them.)

Scene 4. In Olivia's garden. Olivia sends for Malvolio; Maria hints that he is very strange in his manner. Malvolio appears, dressed in a peculiar way, and behaves as if he were Olivia's lover—to the amazement of Olivia. Believing him to be really affected in his head, Olivia hands him over to the care of Sir Toby, who carries the scheme against Malvolio a step further and has him shut up in a dark room.

We then pass to the proposed duel between Sir Andrew and Viola. Each is really afraid to fight, but Sir Toby and Fabian urge them on; and then, just when they are about to draw their swords, Antonio enters, mistakes Viola (Cesario) for Sebastian, and wishes to fight in Viola's place with Sir Andrew. Antonio, however, is now arrested by officers of Orsino. In his difficulty he appeals to Viola for the purse lent to Sebastian, and more confusions arise through the resemblance of the twins.

Act IV., Scene 1. Near Olivia's house. The Clown meets Sebastian and supposes him to be Cesario (Viola). Sir Andrew and Sir Toby entering make a similar mistake, and Sir Andrew resumes (as he thinks) the quarrel with Cesario which Antonio interrupted. Olivia comes on the scene, repeats, of course, the mistake made by Sir Andrew and Sir Toby, whom she bids leave her, and asks Sebastian to go into the house with her. He consents, wondering what it all means.

Scene 2. At Olivia's house. Malvolio has been confined by Sir Toby in a dark room because of his supposed madness. The Clown visits and talks with him, first in the assumed character of a clergyman, then in his own person. The Clown agrees to take a letter from Malvolio to Olivia. (This letter, given to Olivia in Act v., explains the complications connected with the scheme against Malvolio; we feel now that the underplot has been nearly worked out.)

Scene 3. In Olivia's garden. Sebastian expresses his amazement at Olivia's conduct towards him—a stranger to her. Then Olivia enters, with a priest, and begs Sebastian —Cesario, as she thinks—that they may be "betrothed" to each other. He agrees—no doubt astonished at, yet not resenting, a wife. She (still thinking him Cesario) must be equally surprised.

Act V. Near Olivia's house. The complications of plot and underplot are cleared up. Viola and Sebastian meet in the presence of most of the characters of the play, and the resemblance between them explains all difficulties. Olivia finds that she has been "betrothed" to Sebastian, not to Cesario, and is content with the exchange. Orsino, as he cannot win Olivia, transfers his love to Viola. Malvolio's letter is delivered to Olivia (who in the distraction of her love-affairs had forgotten all about him), and she sends for him. At his entrance Fabian explains the trick played upon Malvolio, and adds that as a reward for her cleverness Sir Toby has married Maria.

In considering the structure of the play we should note how important to the plot the notion of mistaken identity

becomes during the last two Acts. The effect of the confusion produced by the resemblance between Sebastian
and Viola runs throughout these two Acts, the scene of
"the dark room" (IV. 2) alone excepted.

VIII

I am glad to have an opportunity of adding now (1903)
some remarks in the fine work on Shakespeare by the
Danish critic, Brandes (English translation, 1898):

> *Twelfth Night* is perhaps the most graceful and harmonious
> comedy Shakespeare ever wrote. It is certainly that in which
> all the notes the poet strikes, the note of seriousness and of
> raillery, of passion, of tenderness, and of laughter, blend in the
> richest and fullest concord. It is like a symphony in which no
> strain can be dispensed with, or is like a picture veiled in a golden
> haze, into which all the colours resolve themselves....
>
> Schlegel made long ago the penetrating observation that, in
> the opening speech of *Twelfth Night*, Shakespeare reminds us
> how the same word, "fancy," was applied in his day both to
> love and to fancy in the modern sense of the term; whence the
> critic argued, not without ingenuity, that love, regarded as an
> affair of the imagination rather than of the heart, is the
> fundamental theme running through all the variations of the
> play....
>
> While Olivia is sighing in vain for Viola, she necessarily
> appears as though seized with a mild erotic madness, similar to
> that of the Duke: and the folly of each is parodied in a witty
> and delightful fashion by Malvolio's entirely ludicrous love for
> his mistress, and vain confidence that she returns it. Olivia
> feels and says this of herself, when she exclaims—"Go call him
> hither" etc. (III. 4. 15, 16).

This parody is part of the balance and symmetry of the
play's structure.

Dr Brandes notes that the incident of Olivia falling in
love with Orsino's disguised messenger finds a close parallel
in a Spanish novel, entitled *Diana* (well known to the
Elizabethans through a translation), by the Portuguese
writer Montemayor.

The Malvolio-element has always been the main source
of the popularity of *Twelfth Night*, especially as regards

the theatre; and Dr Brandes reminds us that the set of complimentary verses prefixed to the 1640 edition of Shakespeare's Poems, in referring to the dramatist's most popular characters, mentions only three from the Comedies —thus:

> "let but *Beatrice*
> And *Benedicke* be seene, loe in a trice
> The Cockpit, Galleries, Boxes, all are full
> To hear *Malvoglio*, that crosse garter'd Gull."

TWELFTH NIGHT

OR

WHAT YOU WILL

DRAMATIS PERSONÆ.

ORSINO, Duke of Illyria.
SEBASTIAN, brother to Viola.
ANTONIO, a sea captain, friend to Sebastian.
A Sea Captain, friend to Viola.
VALENTINE, ⎫
CURIO, ⎰ gentlemen attending on the Duke.
SIR TOBY BELCH, uncle to Olivia.
SIR ANDREW AGUECHEEK.
MALVOLIO, steward to Olivia.
FABIAN, ⎫
FESTE, a clown, ⎰ servants to Olivia.

OLIVIA.
VIOLA.
MARIA, Olivia's woman.

Lords, a Priest, Sailors, Officers, Musicians,
and Attendants.

SCENE
A city in Illyria, and the sea-coast near it.

TWELFTH NIGHT

OR

WHAT YOU WILL

ACT I.

SCENE I. *The* Duke's *Palace.*

Enter Duke, CURIO, *and other* Lords; Musicians *attending.*

Duke. If music be the food of love, play on;
Give me excess of it, that, surfeiting,
The appetite may sicken, and so die.
That strain again! it had a dying fall:
O, it came o'er my ear like the sweet sound
That breathes upon a bank of violets,
Stealing and giving odour! Enough; no more:
'Tis not so sweet now as it was before.
O spirit of love, how quick and fresh art thou!
That, notwithstanding thy capacity   10
Receiveth as the sea, nought enters there,
Of what validity and pitch soe'er,
But falls into abatement and low price,
Even in a minute! so full of shapes is fancy,
That it alone is high fantastical.
    Curio. Will you go hunt, my lord?
    Duke.   What, Curio?
    Curio. The hart.
    Duke. Why, so I do, the noblest that I have:
O, when mine eyes did see Olivia first,
Methought she purg'd the air of pestilence!   20
That instant was I turn'd into a hart;
And my desires, like fell and cruel hounds,
E'er since pursue me.

Enter VALENTINE.

How now! what news from her?
Valentine. So please my lord, I might not be admitted;
But from her handmaid do return this answer:
The element itself, till seven years' heat,
Shall not behold her face at ample view;
But, like a cloistress, she will veiled walk,
And water once a day her chamber round
30 With eye-offending brine: all this to season
A brother's dead love, which she would keep fresh
And lasting in her sad remembrance.
    Duke. O, she that hath a heart of that fine frame
To pay this debt of love but to a brother,
How will she love, when the rich golden shaft
Hath kill'd the flock of all affections else
That live in her; when liver, brain, and heart,
These sovereign thrones, are all supplied, and fill'd
Her sweet perfections, with one self king!
40 Away before me to sweet beds of flowers:
Love-thoughts lie rich when canopied with bowers.
                                        [*Exeunt.*

SCENE II. *The sea-coast.*

Enter VIOLA, *a* Captain, *and* Sailors.

Viola. What country, friends, is this?
Captain.   This is Illyria, lady.
Viola. And what should I do in Illyria?
My brother he is in Elysium.
Perchance he is not drown'd: what think you, sailors?
Captain. It is perchance that you yourself were sav'd.
Viola. O my poor brother! and so perchance may he be.
Captain. True, madam: and, to comfort you with
Assure yourself, after our ship did split,   [chance,
10 When you, and those poor number sav'd with you,
Hung on our driving boat, I saw your brother,

Most provident in peril, bind himself—
Courage and hope both teaching him the practice—
To a strong mast that liv'd upon the sea;
Where, like Arion on the dolphin's back,
I saw him hold acquaintance with the waves
So long as I could see.

Viola.   For saying so, there's gold:
Mine own escape unfoldeth to my hope,
Whereto thy speech serves for authority,   20
The like of him. Know'st thou this country?

Captain. Ay, madam, well; for I was bred and born
Not three hours' travel from this very place.

Viola. Who governs here?

Captain. A noble duke, in nature as in name.

Viola. What is his name?

Captain. Orsino.

Viola. Orsino! I have heard my father name him:
He was a bachelor then.

Captain. And so is now, or was so very late;   30
For but a month ago I went from hence,
And then 'twas fresh in murmur,—as, you know,
What great ones do the less will prattle of,—
That he did seek the love of fair Olivia.

Viola. What's she?

Captain. A virtuous maid, the daughter of a count
That died some twelvemonth since; then leaving her
In the protection of his son, her brother,
Who shortly also died: for whose dear love,
They say, she hath abjur'd the company   40
And sight of men.

Viola.   O that I serv'd that lady,
And might not be deliver'd to the world,
Till I had made mine own occasion mellow,
What my estate is!

Captain.   That were hard to compass;
Because she will admit no kind of suit,
No, not the duke's.

Viola. There is a fair behaviour in thee, captain;
And though that nature with a beauteous wall
Doth oft close in pollution, yet of thee
50 I will believe thou hast a mind that suits
With this thy fair and outward character.
I prithee,—and I'll pay thee bounteously,—
Conceal me what I am; and be my aid
For such disguise as haply shall become
The form of my intent. I'll serve this duke:
Thou shalt present me as an eunuch to him:
It may be worth thy pains; for I can sing,
And speak to him in many sorts of music,
That will allow me very worth his service.
60 What else may hap, to time I will commit;
Only shape thou thy silence to my wit.
    Captain. Be you his eunuch, and your mute I'll be:
When my tongue blabs, then let mine eyes not see.
    Viola. I thank thee: lead me on.   [*Exeunt.*

Scene III. Olivia's *house.*

Enter Sir Toby Belch *and* Maria.

Sir Toby. What a plague means my niece, to take the
death of her brother thus? I am sure care's an enemy
to life.

Maria. By my troth, Sir Toby, you must come in
earlier o' nights: your cousin, my lady, takes great
exceptions to your ill hours.

Sir Toby. Why, let her except before excepted.

Maria. Ay, but you must confine yourself within the
modest limits of order.

10 *Sir Toby.* Confine! I'll confine myself no finer than
I am: these clothes are good enough to drink in; and
so be these boots too,—an they be not, let them hang
themselves in their own straps.

Maria. That quaffing and drinking will undo you: I
heard my lady talk of it yesterday; and of a foolish

knight that you brought in one night here to be her wooer.

Sir Toby. Who, Sir Andrew Aguecheek?

Maria. Ay, he.

Sir Toby. He's as tall a man as any's in Illyria.   20

Maria. What's that to the purpose?

Sir Toby. Why, he has three thousand ducats a year.

Maria. Ay, but he'll have but a year in all these ducats: he's a very fool and a prodigal.

Sir Toby. Fie, that you'll say so! he plays o' the viol-de-gamboys, and speaks three or four languages word for word without book, and hath all the good gifts of nature.

Maria. He hath, indeed, almost natural: for, besides 30 that he's a fool, he's a great quarreller; and, but that he hath the gift of a coward to allay the gust he hath in quarrelling, 'tis thought among the prudent he would quickly have the gift of a grave.

Sir Toby. By this hand, they are scoundrels and sub-stractors that say so of him. Who are they?

Maria. They that add, moreover, he's drunk nightly in your company.

Sir Toby. With drinking healths to my niece: I'll drink 40 to her as long as there is a passage in my throat and drink in Illyria: he's a coward and a coystril that will not drink to my niece till his brains turn o' the toe like a parish-top. What, wench! *Castiliano vulgo;* for here comes Sir Andrew Agueface.

Enter Sir ANDREW AGUECHEEK.

Sir Andrew. Sir Toby Belch! how now, Sir Toby Belch!

Sir Toby. Sweet Sir Andrew!

Sir Andrew. Bless you, fair shrew.   50

Maria. And you too, sir.

Sir Toby. Accost, Sir Andrew, accost.

Sir Andrew. What's that?

Sir Toby. My niece's chambermaid.

Sir Andrew. Good Mistress Accost, I desire better acquaintance.

Maria. My name is Mary, sir.

Sir Andrew. Good Mistress Mary Accost,—

Sir Toby. You mistake, knight: "accost" is front her,
60 woo her.

Sir Andrew. By my troth, I would not in this company. Is that the meaning of "accost"?

Maria. Fare you well, gentlemen.

Sir Toby. An thou let part so, Sir Andrew, would thou mightst never draw sword again.

Sir Andrew. An you part so, mistress, I would I might never draw sword again. Fair lady, do you think you have fools in hand?

70 *Maria.* Sir, I have not you by the hand.

Sir Andrew. Marry, but you shall have: and here's my hand.

Maria. Now, sir, thought is free: I pray you, bring your hand to the buttery-bar, and let it drink.

Sir Andrew. Wherefore, sweet-heart? what's your metaphor?

Maria. It's dry, sir.

Sir Andrew. Why, I think so: I am not such an ass
80 but I can keep my hand dry. But what's your jest?

Maria. A dry jest, sir.

Sir Andrew. Are you full of them?

Maria. Ay, sir, I have them at my fingers' ends: marry, now I let go your hand, I am barren.   [*Exit.*

Sir Toby. O knight, thou lackest a cup of canary: when did I see thee so put down?

Sir Andrew. Never in your life, I think; unless you see canary put me down. Methinks sometimes I have no more wit than a Christian or an ordinary man has:
90 but I am a great eater of beef, and I believe that does harm to my wit.

Sir Toby. No question.

Sir Andrew. An I thought that, I'd forswear it. I'll ride home to-morrow, Sir Toby.

Sir Toby. *Pourquoi*, my dear knight?

Sir Andrew. What is "*pourquoi*"? do or not do? I would I had bestowed that time in the tongues that I have in fencing, dancing, and bear-baiting: O had I but followed the arts!

Sir Toby. Then hadst thou had an excellent head of 100 hair.

Sir Andrew. Why, would that have mended my hair?

Sir Toby. Past question; for thou seest it will not curl by nature.

Sir Andrew. But it becomes me well enough, does't not?

Sir Toby. Excellent; it hangs like flax on a distaff; and I hope to see a housewife take thee and spin it off.   110

Sir Andrew. Faith, I'll home to-morrow, Sir Toby: your niece will not be seen; or if she be, it's four to one she'll none of me: the count himself here hard by woos her.

Sir Toby. She'll none o' the count: she'll not match above her degree, neither in estate, years, nor wit; I have heard her swear't. Tut, there's life in't, man.

Sir Andrew. I'll stay a month longer. I am a fellow o' the strangest mind i' the world; I delight in masques 120 and revels sometimes altogether.

Sir Toby. Art thou good at these kickshawses, knight?

Sir Andrew. As any man in Illyria, whatsoever he be, under the degree of my betters; and yet I will not compare with an old man.

Sir Toby. What is thy excellence in a galliard, knight?

Sir Andrew. Faith, I can cut a caper.

Sir Toby. And I can cut the mutton to't.   130

Sir Andrew. And I think I have the back-trick simply as strong as any man in Illyria.

Sir Toby. Wherefore are these things hid? wherefore have these gifts a curtain before 'em? are they like to take

dust, like Mistress Mall's picture? why dost thou not go
to church in a galliard, and come home in a coranto?
My very walk should be a jig. What dost thou mean?
140 is it a world to hide virtues in? I did think, by the
excellent constitution of thy leg, it was formed under the
star of a galliard.

    Sir Andrew. Ay, 'tis strong, and does indifferent well
in a flame-coloured stock. Shall we set about some revels?

    Sir Toby. What shall we do else? were we not born
under Taurus?

    Sir Andrew. Taurus! that's sides and heart.

    Sir Toby. No, sir; it is legs and thighs. Let me see
150 thee caper [*Sir Andrew dances*]: ha! higher: ha, ha!—
excellent!   [*Exeunt.*

Scene IV. *The* Duke's *Palace.*

Enter Valentine, *and* Viola *in man's attire.*

    Valentine. If the duke continue these favours towards
you, Cesario, you are like to be much advanced: he hath
known you but three days, and already you are no stranger.

    Viola. You either fear his humour or my negligence,
that you call in question the continuance of his love: is
he inconstant, sir, in his favours?

    Valentine. No, believe me.

    Viola. I thank you. Here comes the count.

Enter Duke, Curio, *and* Attendants.

10   *Duke.* Who saw Cesario, ho?

    Viola. On your attendance, my lord; here.

    Duke. Stand you awhile aloof.—Cesario,
Thou know'st no less but all; I have unclasp'd
To thee the book even of my secret soul:
Therefore, good youth, address thy gait unto her;
Be not denied access, stand at her doors,
And tell them, there thy fixed foot shall grow
Till thou have audience.

Viola.   Sure, my noble lord,
If she be so abandon'd to her sorrow
As it is spoke, she never will admit me.   20
Duke. Be clamorous, and leap all civil bounds,
Rather than make unprofited return.
Viola. Say I do speak with her, my lord, what then?
Duke. O, then unfold the passion of my love,
Surprise her with discourse of my dear faith!
It shall become thee well to act my woes;
She will attend it better in thy youth
Than in a nuncio of more grave aspect.
Viola. I think not so, my lord.
Duke.   Dear lad, believe it;
For they shall yet belie thy happy years,   30
That say thou art a man: Diana's lip
Is not more smooth and rubious; thy small pipe
Is as the maiden's organ, shrill and sound,
And all is semblative a woman's part.
I know thy constellation is right apt
For this affair. Some four or five attend him;
All, if you will; for I myself am best
When least in company. Prosper well in this,
And thou shalt live as freely as thy lord
To call his fortunes thine.
Viola.   I'll do my best   40
To woo your lady:—[*Aside*] yet, a barful strife!
Whoe'er I woo, myself would be his wife.   [*Exeunt.*

SCENE V. OLIVIA'S *house.*

Enter MARIA *and* Clown.

Maria. Nay, either tell me where thou hast been, or
I will not open my lips so wide as a bristle may enter,
in way of thy excuse: my lady will hang thee for thy
absence.

Clown. Let her hang me: he that is well hanged in
this world needs to fear no colours.

Maria. Make that good.

Clown. He shall see none to fear.

Maria. A good lenten answer: I can tell thee where
10 that saying was born, of "I fear no colours."

Clown. Where, good Mistress Mary?

Maria. In the wars; and that may you be bold to say
in your foolery.

Clown. Well, God give them wisdom that have it;
and those that are fools, let them use their talents.

Maria. Yet you will be hanged for being so long
absent; or, to be turned away,—is not that as good as a
hanging to you?

20 *Clown.* Many a good hanging prevents a bad marriage;
and, for turning away, let summer bear it out.

Maria. You are resolute, then?

Clown. Not so, neither; but I am resolved on two
points.

Maria. That if one break, the other will hold; or, if
both break, your gaskins fall.

Clown. Apt, in good faith; very apt. Well, go thy
way; if Sir Toby would leave drinking, thou wert as
witty a piece of Eve's flesh as any in Illyria.

32 *Maria.* Peace, you rogue, no more o' that. Here comes
my lady: make your excuse wisely, you were best. [*Exit.*

Clown. Wit, an't be thy will, put me into good fooling!
Those wits, that think they have thee, do very oft prove
fools; and I, that am sure I lack thee, may pass for a wise
man: for what says Quinapalus? "Better a witty fool
40 than a foolish wit."

Enter OLIVIA *and* MALVOLIO.

God bless thee, lady!

Olivia. Take the fool away.

Clown. Do you not hear, fellows? Take away the lady.

Olivia. Go to, you're a dry fool; I'll no more of you:
besides, you grow dishonest.

Clown. Two faults, madonna, that drink and good

counsel will amend: for give the dry fool drink, then is the
fool not dry: bid the dishonest man mend himself; if 50
he mend, he is no longer dishonest; if he cannot, let
the botcher mend him: any thing that's mended is but
patched: virtue that transgresses is but patched with sin;
and sin that amends is but patched with virtue: if that
this simple syllogism will serve, so; if it will not, what
remedy? The lady bade take away the fool; therefore, I say
again, take her away.

Olivia. Sir, I bade them take away you. 60

Clown. Misprision in the highest degree! Lady, *cucullus non facit monachum*; that's as much to say as I wear
not motley in my brain. Good madonna, give me leave
to prove you a fool.

Olivia. Can you do it?

Clown. Dexteriously, good madonna.

Olivia. Make your proof.

Clown. I must catechize you for it, madonna: good
my mouse of virtue, answer me.

Olivia. Well, sir, for want of other idleness, I'll bide 70
your proof.

Clown. Good madonna, why mournest thou?

Olivia. Good fool, for my brother's death.

Clown. I think his soul is in hell, madonna.

Olivia. I know his soul is in heaven, fool.

Clown. The more fool, madonna, to mourn for your
brother's soul being in heaven.—Take away the fool,
gentlemen.

Olivia. What think you of this fool, Malvolio? doth
he not mend? 80

Malvolio. Yes, and shall do till the pangs of death
shake him: infirmity, that decays the wise, doth ever
make the better fool.

Clown. God send you, sir, a speedy infirmity, for the
better increasing your folly! Sir Toby will be sworn that
I am no fox; but he will not pass his word for twopence
that you are no fool.

Olivia. How say you to that, Malvolio?

Malvolio. I marvel your ladyship takes delight in
90 such a barren rascal: I saw him put down the other
day with an ordinary fool that has no more brain than
a stone. Look you now, he's out of his guard already;
unless you laugh and minister occasion to him, he is
gagged. I protest, I take these wise men, that crow
so at these set kind of fools, no better than the fools'
zanies.

Olivia. O, you are sick of self-love, Malvolio, and taste
with a distempered appetite. To be generous, guiltless,
100 and of free disposition, is to take those things for bird-
bolts that you deem cannon-bullets: there is no slander
in an allowed fool, though he do nothing but rail; nor
no railing in a known discreet man, although he do
nothing but reprove.

Clown. Now Mercury endue thee with leasing, for
thou speakest well of fools!

Re-enter MARIA.

Maria. Madam, there is at the gate a young gentleman
much desires to speak with you.

Olivia. From the Count Orsino, is it?

110 *Maria.* I know not, madam: 'tis a fair young man,
and well attended.

Olivia. Who of my people hold him in delay?

Maria. Sir Toby, madam, your kinsman.

Olivia. Fetch him off, I pray you; he speaks nothing
but madman: fie on him! [*Exit Maria.*] Go you, Malvolio: if it be a suit from the count, I am sick, or not at
home; what you will, to dismiss it. [*Exit Malvolio.*] Now
you see, sir, how your fooling grows old, and people
dislike it.

120 *Clown.* Thou hast spoke for us, madonna, as if thy
eldest son should be a fool,—whose skull Jove cram with
brains! for here he comes, one of thy kin, has a most
weak *pia mater.*

Enter Sir TOBY.

Olivia. By mine honour, half drunk.—What is he at the gate, cousin?

Sir Toby. A gentleman.

Olivia. A gentleman! what gentleman?

Sir Toby. 'Tis a gentleman here—a plague o' these pickle-herring! How now, sot!

Clown. Good Sir Toby!   130

Olivia. Cousin, cousin, how have you come so early by this lethargy?—

Sir Toby. There's one at the gate.

Olivia. Ay, marry, what is he?

Sir Toby. Let him be the devil, an he will, I care not: give me faith, say I. Well, it's all one.   [*Exit.*

Olivia. What's a drunken man like, fool?

Clown. Like a drowned man, a fool, and a madman: one draught above heat makes him a fool; the second 140 mads him; and a third drowns him.

Olivia. Go thou and seek the crowner, and let him sit o' my coz; for he's in the third degree of drink,— he's drowned: go, look after him.

Clown. He is but mad yet, madonna; and the fool shall look to the madman.   [*Exit.*

Re-enter MALVOLIO.

Malvolio. Madam, yond young fellow swears he will speak with you. I told him you were sick; he takes on him to understand so much, and therefore comes to speak 150 with you: I told him you were asleep; he seems to have a foreknowledge of that too, and therefore comes to speak with you. What is to be said to him, lady? he's fortified against any denial.

Olivia. Tell him he shall not speak with me.

Malvolio. He has been told so; and he says, he'll stand at your door like a sheriff's post, and be the supporter to a bench, but he'll speak with you.

Olivia. What kind o' man is he?

160 *Malvolio.* Why, of mankind.

Olivia. What manner of man?

Malvolio. Of very ill manner; he'll speak with you, will you or no.

Olivia. Of what personage and years is he?

Malvolio. Not yet old enough for a man, nor young enough for a boy; as a squash is before 'tis a peascod, or a codling when 'tis almost an apple: 'tis with him in standing water, between boy and man. He is very well-170 favoured, and he speaks very shrewishly; one would think his mother's milk were scarce out of him.

Olivia. Let him approach: call in my gentlewoman.

Malvolio. Gentlewoman, my lady calls.   [*Exit.*

Re-enter MARIA.

Olivia. Give me my veil: come, throw it o'er my face. We'll once more hear Orsino's embassy.

Enter VIOLA.

Viola. The honourable lady of the house, which is she?

180 *Olivia.* Speak to me; I shall answer for her. Your will?

Viola. Most radiant, exquisite, and unmatchable beauty,—I pray you, tell me if this be the lady of the house, for I never saw her: I would be loth to cast away my speech; for, besides that it is excellently well penned, I have taken great pains to con it. Good beauties, let me sustain no scorn; I am very comptible, even to the least sinister usage.

Olivia. Whence came you, sir?

190 *Viola.* I can say little more than I have studied, and that question's out of my part. Good gentle one, give me modest assurance if you be the lady of the house, that I may proceed in my speech.

Olivia. Are you a comedian?

Viola. No, my profound heart: and yet, by the very

fangs of malice I swear I am not that I play. Are you
the lady of the house?

Olivia. If I do not usurp myself, I am.

Viola. Most certain, if you are she, you do usurp
yourself; for what is yours to bestow is not yours to 200
reserve. But this is from my commission: I will on with
my speech in your praise, and then show you the heart
of my message.

Olivia. Come to what is important in't: I forgive you
the praise.

Viola. Alas, I took great pains to study it, and 'tis
poetical.

Olivia. It is the more like to be feigned: I pray you,
keep it in. I heard you were saucy at my gates; and 210
allowed your approach rather to wonder at you than to
hear you. If you be not mad, be gone; if you have reason,
be brief: 'tis not that time of moon with me to make one
in so skipping a dialogue.

Maria. Will you hoist sail, sir? here lies your way.

Viola. No, good swabber; I am to hull here a little
longer.—Some mollification for your giant, sweet lady.
Tell me your mind: I am a messenger.   220

Olivia. Sure, you have some hideous matter to deliver,
when the courtesy of it is so fearful. Speak your
office.

Viola. It alone concerns your ear. I bring no overture
of war, no taxation of homage: I hold the olive in my
hand; my words are as full of peace as matter.

Olivia. Yet you began rudely. What are you? what
would you?

Viola. The rudeness that hath appeared in me have I 230
learned from my entertainment. What I am, and what I
would, are secret: to your ears, divinity; to any other's,
profanation.

Olivia. Give us the place alone: we will hear this
divinity. [*Exit Maria.*] Now, sir, what is your text?

Viola. Most sweet lady,—

Olivia. A comfortable doctrine, and much may be said
240 of it. Where lies your text?

Viola. In Orsino's bosom.

Olivia. In his bosom! In what chapter of his bosom?

Viola. To answer by the method, in the first of his
heart.

Olivia. O, I have read it: it is heresy. Have you no
more to say?

Viola. Good madam, let me see your face.

Olivia. Have you any commission from your lord to
250 negotiate with my face? You are now out of your text:
but we will draw the curtain, and show you the picture.
Look you, sir, such a one I was this present: is't not
well done?   [*Unveiling.*

Viola. Excellently done, if God did all.

Olivia. 'Tis in grain, sir; 'twill endure wind and
weather.

Viola. 'Tis beauty truly blent, whose red and white
Nature's own sweet and cunning hand laid on:
Lady, you are the cruell'st she alive,
260 If you will lead these graces to the grave
And leave the world no copy.

Olivia. O, sir, I will not be so hard-hearted; I will
give out divers schedules of my beauty: it shall be in-
ventoried, and every particle and utensil labelled to my
will:—as, item, two lips, indifferent red; item, two gray
eyes, with lids to them; item, one neck, one chin, and
so forth. Were you sent hither to praise me?

Viola. I see you what you are,—you are too proud;
270 But, if you were the devil, you are fair.
My lord and master loves you: O, such love
Could be but recompens'd, though you were crown'd
The nonpareil of beauty!

Olivia.   How does he love me?

Viola. With adorations, fertile tears,
With groans that thunder love, with sighs of fire.

Oli. Your lord does know my mind; I cannot love him:

Yet I suppose him virtuous, know him noble,
Of great estate, of fresh and stainless youth;
In voices well divulg'd, free, learn'd, and valiant;
And in dimension and the shape of nature   280
A gracious person: but yet I cannot love him;
He might have took his answer long ago.

    Viola. If I did love you in my master's flame,
With such a suffering, such a deadly life,
In your denial I would find no sense;
I would not understand it.

    Olivia.   Why, what would you?

    Viola. Make me a willow cabin at your gate,
And call upon my soul within the house;
Write loyal cantons of contemned love,
And sing them loud even in the dead of night;   290
Holla your name to the reverberate hills,
And make the babbling gossip of the air
Cry out, "Olivia!" O, you should not rest
Between the elements of air and earth,
But you should pity me!

    Olivia. You might do much. What is your parentage?

    Viola. Above my fortunes, yet my state is well:
I am a gentleman.

    Olivia.   Get you to your lord;
I cannot love him: let him send no more;
Unless, perchance, you come to me again,
To tell me how he takes it. Fare you well: 300
I thank you for your pains: spend this for me.

    Viola. I am no fee'd post, lady; keep your purse:
My master, not myself, lacks recompense.
Love make his heart of flint that you shall love;
And let your fervour, like my master's, be
Plac'd in contempt! Farewell, fair cruelty.   [*Exit.*

    Olivia. "What is your parentage?"
"Above my fortunes, yet my state is well:
I am a gentleman." I'll be sworn thou art;   310
Thy tongue, thy face, thy limbs, actions, and spirit,

Do give thee fivefold blazon: not too fast: soft, soft!
Unless the master were the man! How now?
Even so quickly may one catch the plague?
Methinks I feel this youth's perfections
With an invisible and subtle stealth
To creep in at mine eyes. Well, let it be.—
What, ho, Malvolio!

Re-enter MALVOLIO.

Malvolio.   Here, madam, at your service.
Olivia. Run after that same peevish messenger,
320 The county's man: he left this ring behind him,
Would I or not: tell him I'll none of it.
Desire him not to flatter with his lord,
Nor hold him up with hopes; I am not for him:
If that the youth will come this way to-morrow,
I'll give him reasons for't. Hie thee, Malvolio.
Malvolio. Madam, I will.   [*Exit.*
Olivia. I do I know not what; and fear to find
Mine eye too great a flatterer for my mind.
Fate, show thy force: ourselves we do not owe;
330 What is decreed must be,—and be this so!   [*Exit.*

ACT II.

SCENE I. *The sea-coast.*

Enter ANTONIO *and* SEBASTIAN.

Antonio. Will you stay no longer? nor will you not
that I go with you?
Sebastian. By your patience, no. My stars shine darkly
over me: the malignancy of my fate might perhaps distemper yours; therefore I shall crave of you your leave
that I may bear my evils alone: it were a bad recompense
for your love, to lay any of them on you.
Antonio. Let me yet know of you whither you are bound.

Sebastian. No, sooth, sir: my determinate voyage is 11
mere extravagancy. But I perceive in you so excellent a
touch of modesty, that you will not extort from me what
I am willing to keep in; therefore it charges me in
manners the rather to express myself. You must know
of me, then, Antonio, my name is Sebastian, which I
called Roderigo. My father was that Sebastian of
Messaline, whom I know you have heard of. He left
behind him myself and a sister, both born in an hour: 20
if the heavens had been pleased, would we had so
ended! but you, sir, altered that; for some hour before
you took me from the breach of the sea was my sister
drowned.

Antonio. Alas the day!

Sebastian. A lady, sir, though it was said she much
resembled me, was yet of many accounted beautiful: but,
though I could not with such estimable wonder overfar
believe that, yet thus far I will boldly publish her,—she 30
bore a mind that envy could not but call fair. She is
drowned already, sir, with salt water, though I seem to
drown her remembrance again with more.

Antonio. Pardon me, sir, your bad entertainment.

Sebastian. O good Antonio, forgive me your trouble!

Antonio. If you will not murder me for my love, let
me be your servant.

Sebastian. If you will not undo what you have done,
that is, kill him whom you have recovered, desire it not.
Fare ye well at once: my bosom is full of kindness; and 40
I am yet so near the manners of my mother, that, upon
the least occasion more, mine eyes will tell tales of me.
I am bound to the Count Orsino's court: farewell.

[*Exit.*

Antonio. The gentleness of all the gods go with thee!
I have many enemies in Orsino's court,
Else would I very shortly see thee there:
But, come what may, I do adore thee so,
That danger shall seem sport, and I will go.   [*Exit.* 49

Scene II. *A street.*

Enter Viola, Malvolio *following.*

Malvolio. Were not you even now with the Countess
Olivia?

Viola. Even now, sir; on a moderate pace I have
since arrived but hither.

Malvolio. She returns this ring to you, sir: you might
have saved me my pains, to have taken it away yourself.
She adds, moreover, that you should put your lord into
a desperate assurance she will none of him: and one
10 thing more, that you be never so hardy to come again
in his affairs, unless it be to report your lord's taking of
this. Receive it so.

Viola. She took the ring of me: I'll none of it.

Malvolio. Come, sir, you peevishly threw it to her;
and her will is, it should be so returned: if it be worth
stooping for, there it lies in your eye; if not, be it his
that finds it.   [*Exit.*

Viola. I left no ring with her: what means this lady?
Fortune forbid my outside have not charm'd her!
20 She made good view of me; indeed, so much,
That sure methought her eyes had lost her tongue,
For she did speak in starts distractedly.
She loves me, sure; the cunning of her passion
Invites me in this churlish messenger.
None of my lord's ring! why, he sent her none.
I am the man: if it be so,—as 'tis,—
Poor lady, she were better love a dream.
Disguise, I see, thou art a wickedness,
Wherein the pregnant enemy does much.
30 How easy is it for the proper-false
In women's waxen hearts to set their forms!
Alas, our frailty is the cause, not we!
For such as we are made of, such we be.
How will this fadge? my master loves her dearly;

And I, poor monster, fond as much on him;
And she, mistaken, seems to dote on me.
What will become of this? As I am man,
My state is desperate for my master's love;
As I am woman,—now, alas the day!—
What thriftless sighs shall poor Olivia breathe!   40
O Time, thou must untangle this, not I;
It is too hard a knot for me to untie!   [*Exit.*

SCENE III. OLIVIA's *house.*

Enter Sir TOBY *and* Sir ANDREW.

Sir Toby. Approach, Sir Andrew: not to be a-bed
after midnight is to be up betimes; and *diluculo surgere,*
thou know'st,—

Sir Andrew. Nay, by my troth, I know not: but I
know, to be up late is to be up late.

Sir Toby. A false conclusion: I hate it as an unfilled
can. To be up after midnight, and to go to bed then,
is early: so that, to go to bed after midnight is to go to
bed betimes. Does not our life consist of the four elements?   10

Sir Andrew. Faith, so they say; but I think it rather
consists of eating and drinking.

Sir Toby. Thou'rt a scholar: let us therefore eat and
drink.—Marian, I say! a stoup of wine!

Sir Andrew. Here comes the fool, i' faith.

Enter Clown.

Clown. How now, my hearts! did you never see the
picture of "We Three"?

Sir Toby. Welcome, ass. Now let's have a catch.

Sir Andrew. By my troth, the fool has an excellent
breast. I had rather than forty shillings I had such a   20
leg, and so sweet a breath to sing, as the fool has. In
sooth, thou wast in very gracious fooling last night, when
thou spokest of Pigrogromitus, of the Vapians passing the

equinoctial of Queubus: 'twas very good, i' faith. I sent
thee sixpence for thy leman: hadst it?

Clown. I did impeticos thy gratillity; for Malvolio's
nose is no whipstock: my lady has a white hand, and the
Myrmidons are no bottle-ale houses.

30   *Sir Andrew.* Excellent! why, this is the best fooling,
when all is done. Now, a song.

Sir Toby. Come on; there is sixpence for you: let's
have a song.

Sir Andrew. There's a testril of me too: if one knight
give a—

Clown. Would you have a love-song, or a song of
good life?

Sir Toby. A love-song, a love-song.

Sir Andrew. Ay, ay: I care not for good life.

Song.

40   *Clown.*   O mistress mine, where are you roaming?
            O, stay and hear; your true love's coming,
               That can sing both high and low:
            Trip no further, pretty sweeting;
            Journeys end in lovers meeting,
               Every wise man's son doth know.

Sir And. Excellent good, i' faith.

Sir Toby. Good, good.

Clown.   What is love? 'tis not hereafter;
            Present mirth hath present laughter;
50   What's to come is still unsure:
            In delay there lies no plenty;
            Then come kiss me, sweet and twenty,
               Youth's a stuff will not endure.

Sir Andrew. A mellifluous voice, as I am true
knight.

Sir Toby. A contagious breath.

Sir Andrew. Very sweet and contagious, i' faith.

Sir Toby. To hear by the nose, it is dulcet in con-
tagion. But shall we make the welkin dance indeed?

shall we rouse the night-owl in a catch that will draw 60
three souls out of one weaver? shall we do that?

Sir Andrew. An you love me, let's do't: I am dog at
a catch.

Clown. By'r lady, sir, and some dogs will catch well.

Sir Andrew. Most certain. Let our catch be, "Thou
knave."

Clown. "Hold thy peace, thou knave," knight? I shall
be constrained in't to call thee knave, knight.   70

Sir Andrew. 'Tis not the first time I have constrained
one to call me knave. Begin, fool: it begins, "Hold thy
peace."

Clown. I shall never begin, if I hold my peace.

Sir Andrew. Good, i' faith. Come, begin.

                              [*They sing the catch.*

Enter MARIA.

Maria. What a caterwauling do you keep here! If my
lady have not called up her steward Malvolio and bid him
turn you out of doors, never trust me.

Sir Toby. My lady's a Catalan, we are politicians, 80
Malvolio's a Peg-a-Ramsey, and "Three merry men be
we." Am not I consanguineous? am I not of her blood?
Tilly-vally, lady! [*Sings.*] "There dwelt a man in Baby-
lon, lady, lady!"

Clown. Beshrew me, the knight's in admirable fooling.

Sir Andrew. Ay, he does well enough if he be dis-
posed, and so do I too: he does it with a better grace,
but I do it more natural.

Sir Toby. [*Sings.*] "O, the twelfth day of December,"—

Maria. For the love o' God, peace!   92

Enter MALVOLIO.

Malvolio. My masters, are you mad? or what are you?
Have you no wit, manners, nor honesty, but to gabble
like tinkers at this time of night? Do you make an ale-
house of my lady's house, that ye squeak out your

coziers' catches without any mitigation or remorse of
voice? Is there no respect of place, persons, nor time,
in you?

100   *Sir Toby.* We did keep time, sir, in our catches.
Sneck up!

Malvolio. Sir Toby, I must be round with you. My
lady bade me tell you, that, though she harbours you as
her kinsman, she's nothing allied to your disorders. If
you can separate yourself and your misdemeanours, you
are welcome to the house; if not, an it would please
you to take leave of her, she is very willing to bid you
farewell.

Sir Toby. "Farewell, dear heart, since I must needs be
110 gone."

Maria. Nay, good Sir Toby.

Clown. "His eyes do show his days are almost
done."

Malvolio. Is't even so?

Sir Toby. "But I will never die."

Clown. Sir Toby, there you lie.

Malvolio. This is much credit to you.

Sir Toby. "Shall I bid him go?"

Clown. "What an if you do?"

120   *Sir Toby.* "Shall I bid him go, and spare not?"

Clown. "O, no, no, no, no, you dare not."

Sir Toby. Out o' tune, sir? ye lie.—Art any more than
a steward? Dost thou think, because thou art virtuous,
there shall be no more cakes and ale?

Clown. Yes, by Saint Anne; and ginger shall be hot
i' the mouth too.

Sir Toby. Thou'rt i' the right.—Go, sir, rub your chain
with crumbs.—A stoup of wine, Maria!

130   *Malvolio.* Mistress Mary, if you prized my lady's
favour at any thing more than contempt, you would not
give means for this uncivil rule: she shall know of it, by
this hand.   [*Exit.*

Maria. Go shake your ears.

Sir Andrew. 'Twere as good a deed as to drink when a man's a-hungry, to challenge him the field, and then to break promise with him, and make a fool of him.

Sir Toby. Do't, knight: I'll write thee a challenge; or I'll deliver thy indignation to him by word of mouth.

Maria. Sweet Sir Toby, be patient for to-night: since 142 the youth of the count's was to-day with my lady, she is much out of quiet. For Monsieur Malvolio, let me alone with him: if I do not gull him into a nayword, and make him a common recreation, do not think I have wit enough to lie straight in my bed: I know I can do it.

Sir Toby. Possess us, possess us; tell us something of him. 150

Maria. Marry, sir, sometimes he is a kind of puritan.

Sir Andrew. O, if I thought that, I'd beat him like a dog!

Sir Toby. What, for being a puritan? thy exquisite reason, dear knight?

Sir Andrew. I have no exquisite reason for't, but I have reason good enough.

Maria. The devil a puritan that he is, or any thing constantly, but a time-pleaser; an affectioned ass, that 160 cons state without book, and utters it by great swarths: the best persuaded of himself, so crammed, as he thinks, with excellencies, that it is his grounds of faith that all that look on him love him; and on that vice in him will my revenge find notable cause to work.

Sir Toby. What wilt thou do?

Maria. I will drop in his way some obscure epistles of love; wherein, by the colour of his beard, the shape 170 of his leg, the manner of his gait, the expressure of his eye, forehead, and complexion, he shall find himself most feelingly personated: I can write very like my lady, your niece; on a forgotten matter we can hardly make distinction of our hands.

Sir Toby. Excellent! I smell a device.

Sir Andrew. I have't in my nose too.

Sir Toby. He shall think, by the letters that thou wilt drop, that they come from my niece, and that she's in
180 love with him.

Maria. My purpose is, indeed, a horse of that colour.

Sir Andrew. And your horse now would make him an ass.

Maria. Ass, I doubt not.

Sir Andrew. O, 'twill be admirable!

Maria. Sport royal, I warrant you: I know my physic will work with him. I will plant you two, and let the
190 fool make a third, where he shall find the letter: observe his construction of it. For this night, to bed, and dream on the event. Farewell.   [*Exit.*

Sir Toby. Good night, Penthesilea.

Sir Andrew. Before me, she's a good wench.

Sir Toby. She's a beagle, true-bred, and one that adores me: what o' that?

Sir Andrew. I was adored once too.

Sir Toby. Let's to bed, knight.—Thou hadst need send for more money.

200 *Sir Andrew.* If I cannot recover your niece, I am a foul way out.

Sir Toby. Send for money, knight: if thou hast her not i' the end, call me cut.

Sir Andrew. If I do not, never trust me, take it how you will.

Sir Toby. Come, come; I'll go burn some sack; 'tis too late to go to bed now: come, knight; come, knight.
                    [*Exeunt.*

SCENE IV. *The* Duke's *Palace.*

Enter Duke, VIOLA, CURIO, *and others.*

Duke. Give me some music. Now, good morrow, friends.
Now, good Cesario, but that piece of song,
That old and antique song we heard last night:
Methought it did relieve my passion much,

More than light airs and recollected terms
Of these most brisk and giddy-paced times:
Come, but one verse.

Curio. He is not here, so please your lordship, that
should sing it.

Duke. Who was it?   10

Curio. Feste, the jester, my lord; a fool that the lady
Olivia's father took much delight in: he is about the house.

Duke. Seek him out, and play the tune the while.
                              [*Exit Curio. Music.*
Come hither, boy: if ever thou shalt love,
In the sweet pangs of it remember me;
For such as I am all true lovers are,—
Unstaid and skittish in all motions else,
Save in the constant image of the creature
That is belov'd. How dost thou like this tune?   20

Viola. It gives a very echo to the seat
Where Love is thron'd.

Duke.   Thou dost speak masterly:
My life upon't, young though thou art, thine eye
Hath stay'd upon some favour that it loves;
Hath it not, boy?

Viola.   A little, by your favour.

Duke. What kind of woman is't?

Viola.   Of your complexion.

Duke. She is not worth thee, then. What years, i'

Viola. About your years, my lord.   [faith?

Duke. Too old, by heaven: let still the woman take   30
An elder than herself; so wears she to him,
So sways she level in her husband's heart:
For, boy, however we do praise ourselves,
Our fancies are more giddy and unfirm,
More longing, wavering, sooner lost and worn,
Than women's are.

Viola.   I think it well, my lord.

Duke. Then let thy love be younger than thyself,
Or thy affection cannot hold the bent;

For women are as roses, whose fair flower,
40 Being once display'd, doth fall that very hour.
    Viola. And so they are: alas, that they are so;
To die, even when they to perfection grow!

Re-enter Curio *with* Clown.

    Duke. O, fellow, come, the song we had last night.
Mark it, Cesario; it is old and plain:
The spinsters and the knitters in the sun,
And the free maids that weave their thread with bones,
Do use to chant it: it is silly sooth,
And dallies with the innocence of love,
Like the old age.
50   *Clown.* Are you ready, sir?
    Duke. Ay; prithee, sing.   *[Music.*

Song.

  Clo. Come away, come away, death,
       And in sad cypress let me be laid;
  Fly away, fly away, breath;
       I am slain by a fair cruel maid.
  My shroud of white, stuck all with yew,
       O, prepare it!
  My part of death, no one so true
       Did share it.

60   Not a flower, not a flower sweet,
       On my black coffin let there be strown;
  Not a friend, not a friend greet
       My poor corpse, where my bones shall be
  A thousand thousand sighs to save,   [thrown:
       Lay me, O, where
  Sad true lover never find my grave,
       To weep there!

    Duke. There's for thy pains.
    Clown. No pains, sir; I take pleasure in singing, sir.
71   *Duke.* I'll pay thy pleasure, then.

Clown. Truly, sir, and pleasure will be paid, one time
or another.

Duke. Give me now leave to leave thee.

Clown. Now, the melancholy god protect thee: and
the tailor make thy doublet of changeable taffeta, for thy
mind is a very opal! I would have men of such constancy
put to sea, that their business might be every thing, and
their intent every where; for that's it that always makes 80
a good voyage of nothing. Farewell.   [*Exit.*

Duke. Let all the rest give place.

                      [*Curio and Attendants retire.*

                     Once more, Cesario,

Get thee to yond same sovereign cruelty:
Tell her, my love, more noble than the world,
Prizes not quantity of dirty lands;
The parts that fortune hath bestow'd upon her,
Tell her, I hold as giddily as fortune;
But 'tis that miracle and queen of gems
That nature pranks her in attracts my soul.

Viola. But if she cannot love you, sir?   90

Duke. I cannot be so answer'd.

Viola.   Sooth, but you must.

Say that some lady—as, perhaps, there is—
Hath for your love as great a pang of heart
As you have for Olivia: you cannot love her;
You tell her so; must she not, then, be answer'd?

Duke. There is no woman's sides
Can bide the beating of so strong a passion
As love doth give my heart; no woman's heart
So big, to hold so much; they lack retention.
Alas, their love may be call'd appetite,—   100
No motion of the liver, but the palate,—
That suffer surfeit, cloyment, and revolt;
But mine is all as hungry as the sea,
And can digest as much: make no compare
Between that love a woman can bear me
And that I owe Olivia.

Viola.   Ay, but I know,—

Duke. What dost thou know?

Viola. Too well what love women to men may owe:
In faith, they are as true of heart as we.
110 My father had a daughter lov'd a man,
As it might be, perhaps, were I a woman,
I should your lordship.

Duke.   And what's her history?

Viola. A blank, my lord. She never told her love,
But let concealment, like a worm i' the bud,
Feed on her damask cheek: she pin'd in thought;
And with a green and yellow melancholy
She sat like Patience on a monument,
Smiling at grief. Was not this love indeed?
We men may say more, swear more: but, indeed,
120 Our shows are more than will; for still we prove
Much in our vows, but little in our love.

Duke. But died thy sister of her love, my boy?

Viola. I am all the daughters of my father's house,
And all the brothers too;—and yet I know not.
Sir, shall I to this lady?

Duke.   Ay, that's the theme.
To her in haste; give her this jewel; say,
My love can give no place, bide no denay.   [*Exeunt.*

SCENE V. OLIVIA'S *garden.*

Enter Sir TOBY, Sir ANDREW, *and* FABIAN.

Sir Toby. Come thy ways, Signior Fabian.

Fabian. Nay, I'll come: if I lose a scruple of this sport,
let me be boiled to death with melancholy.

Sir Toby. Wouldst thou not be glad to have the
niggardly rascally sheep-biter come by some notable
shame?

Fabian. I would exult, man: you know he brought
me out o' favour with my lady about a bear-baiting
10 here.

Sir Toby. To anger him, we'll have the bear again; and we will fool him black and blue:—shall we not, Sir Andrew?

Sir Andrew. An we do not, it is pity of our lives.

Sir Toby. Here comes the little villain.

Enter MARIA.

How now, my metal of India!

Maria. Get ye all three into the box-tree: Malvolio's coming down this walk: he has been yonder i' the sun 20 practising behaviour to his own shadow this half hour: observe him, for the love of mockery; for I know this letter will make a contemplative idiot of him. Close, in the name of jesting! Lie thou there [*Throws down a letter*]; for here comes the trout that must be caught with tickling.   [*Exit.*

Enter MALVOLIO.

Malvolio. 'Tis but fortune; all is fortune. Maria once told me she did affect me: and I have heard herself come thus near, that, should she fancy, it should be one of my 30 complexion. Besides, she uses me with a more exalted respect than any one else that follows her. What should I think on't?

Sir Toby. Here's an overweening rogue!

Fabian. O, peace! Contemplation makes a rare turkey-cock of him: how he jets under his advanced plumes!

Sir Andrew. 'Slight, I could so beat the rogue!

Sir Toby. Peace, I say.

Malvolio. To be Count Malvolio,—

Sir Toby. Ah, rogue!   40

Sir Andrew. Pistol him, pistol him.

Sir Toby. Peace, peace!

Malvolio. There is example for't; the lady of the Strachy married the yeoman of the wardrobe.

Sir Andrew. Fie on him, Jezebel!

Fabian. O, peace! now he's deeply in: look how imagination blows him.

Malvolio. Having been three months married to her,
50 sitting in my state,—

Sir Toby. O for a stone-bow, to hit him in the eye!

Malvolio. Calling my officers about me, in my branched velvet gown; having come from Olivia,—

Sir Toby. Fire and brimstone!

Fabian. O, peace, peace!

Malvolio. And then to have the humour of state; and after a demure travel of regard, telling them I know my
60 place, as I would they should do theirs, to ask for my kinsman Toby,—

Sir Toby. Bolts and shackles!

Fabian. O, peace, peace, peace! now, now.

Malvolio. Seven of my people, with an obedient start, make out for him: I frown the while; and perchance wind up my watch, or play with my—some rich jewel. Toby approaches; courtesies there to me,—

Sir Toby. Shall this fellow live?

70 *Fabian.* Though our silence be drawn from us with cars, yet peace.

Malvolio. I extend my hand to him thus, quenching my familiar smile with an austere regard of control,—

Sir Toby. And does not Toby take you a blow o' the lips, then?

Malvolio. Saying, "Cousin Toby, my fortunes having cast me on your niece, give me this prerogative of speech,"—

80 *Sir Toby.* What, what?

Malvolio. "You must amend your drunkenness."

Sir Toby. Out, scab!

Fabian. Nay, patience, or we break the sinews of our plot.

Malvolio. "Besides, you waste the treasure of your time with a foolish knight,"—

Sir Andrew. That's me, I warrant you.

Malvolio. "One Sir Andrew,"—

Sir Andrew. I knew 'twas I; for many do call me fool. 90

Malvolio. What employment have we here?

[*Taking up the letter.*

Fabian. Now is the woodcock near the gin.

Sir Toby. O, peace! and the spirit of humours intimate reading aloud to him!

Malvolio. By my life, this is my lady's hand: these be her very C's, her U's, and her T's; and thus makes she her great P's. It is, in contempt of question, her hand.

Sir Andrew. Her C's, her U's, and her T's: why that? 100

Malvolio. [*Reads*] "To the unknown beloved, this, and my good wishes:" her very phrases!—By your leave, wax.—Soft! and the impressure her Lucrece, with which she uses to seal: 'tis my lady. To whom should this be?

Fabian. This wins him, liver and all.

Mal. [*Reads*] "Jove knows I love:

But who?

Lips, do not move;

No man must know." 110

"No man must know."—What follows? the numbers altered!—"No man must know:"—if this should be thee, Malvolio?

Sir Toby. Marry, hang thee, brock!

Malvolio. [*Reads*]

"I may command where I adore;

But silence, like a Lucrece knife,

With bloodless stroke my heart doth gore:

M, O, A, I, doth sway my life."

Fabian. A fustian riddle!

Sir Toby. Excellent wench, say I. 120

Malvolio. "M, O, A, I, doth sway my life."—Nay, but first, let me see, let me see, let me see.

Fabian. What dish o' poison has she dressed him!

Sir Toby. And with what wing the staniel checks at it!

Malvolio. "I may command where I adore." Why,
she may command me: I serve her; she is my lady.
Why, this is evident to any formal capacity; there is no
130 obstruction in this: and the end,—what should that
alphabetical position portend? if I could make that re-
semble something in me,—Softly! M, O, A, I,—

Sir Toby. O, ay, make up that: he is now at a cold scent.

Fabian. Sowter will cry upon't, for all this, though it
be as rank as a fox.

Malvolio. M,—Malvolio; M,—why, that begins my
name.

Fabian. Did not I say he would work it out? the cur
140 is excellent at faults.

Malvolio. M,—but then there is no consonancy in the
sequel; that suffers under probation: A should follow,
but O does.

Fabian. And O shall end, I hope.

Sir Toby. Ay, or I'll cudgel him, and make him cry O!

Malvolio. And then I comes behind.

Fabian. Ay, an you had any eye behind you, you might
150 see more detraction at your heels than fortunes before you.

Malvolio. M, O, A, I; this simulation is not as the
former: and yet, to crush this a little, it would bow to
me, for every one of these letters are in my name. Soft!
here follows prose.

[*Reads*] "If this fall into thy hand, revolve. In my stars
I am above thee; but be not afraid of greatness: some are
born great, some achieve greatness, and some have
greatness thrust upon 'em. Thy Fates open their hands;
160 let thy blood and spirit embrace them: and, to inure
thyself to what thou art like to be, cast thy humble
slough and appear fresh. Be opposite with a kinsman,
surly with servants; let thy tongue tang arguments of
state; put thyself into the trick of singularity; she thus
advises thee that sighs for thee. Remember who commended thy yellow stockings, and wished to see thee
ever cross-gartered: I say, remember. Go to, thou art

made, if thou desirest to be so; if not, let me see thee
a steward still, the fellow of servants, and not worthy to 170
touch Fortune's fingers Farewell. She that would alter
services with thee,   THE FORTUNATE-UNHAPPY."

Daylight and champain discovers not more: this is open.
I will be proud, I will read politic authors, I will baffle
Sir Toby, I will wash off gross acquaintance, I will be
point-devise the very man. I do not now fool myself, to
let imagination jade me; for every reason excites to this,
that my lady loves me. She did commend my yellow 180
stockings of late, she did praise my leg being cross-
gartered; and in this she manifests herself to my love,
and with a kind of injunction drives me to these habits
of her liking. I thank my stars, I am happy. I will be
strange, stout, in yellow stockings, and cross-gartered,
even with the swiftness of putting on. Jove and my
stars be praised! Here is yet a postscript.
[*Reads*] "Thou canst not choose but know who I am.
If thou entertainest my love, let it appear in thy smiling: 190
thy smiles become thee well; therefore in my presence
still smile, dear my sweet, I prithee."

Jove, I thank thee: I will smile; I will do every thing
that thou wilt have me.   [*Exit.*

Fabian. I will not give my part of this sport for a
pension of thousands to be paid from the Sophy.

Sir Toby. I could marry this wench for this device.

Sir Andrew. So could I too.   200

Sir Toby. And ask no other dowry with her but such
another jest.

Sir Andrew. Nor I neither.

Fabian. Here comes my noble gull-catcher.

Re-enter MARIA.

Sir Toby. Wilt thou set thy foot o' my neck?

Sir Andrew. Or o' mine either?

Sir Toby. Shall I play my freedom at tray-trip, and
become thy bond-slave?

Sir Andrew. I' faith, or I either?

210 *Sir Toby.* Why, thou hast put him in such a dream, that, when the image of it leaves him, he must run mad.

Maria. Nay, but say true; does it work upon him?

Sir Toby. Like aqua-vitæ with a midwife.

Maria. If you will, then, see the fruits of the sport, mark his first approach before my lady: he will come to her in yellow stockings, and 'tis a colour she abhors, and 220 cross-gartered, a fashion she detests; and he will smile upon her, which will now be so unsuitable to her disposition, being addicted to a melancholy as she is, that it cannot but turn him into a notable contempt. If you will see it, follow me.

Sir Toby. To the gates of Tartar, thou most excellent devil of wit!

Sir Andrew. I'll make one too.   [*Exeunt.*

ACT III.

SCENE I. OLIVIA'S *garden.*

Enter VIOLA, *and* Clown *with a tabor.*

Viola. Save thee, friend, and thy music! dost thou live by thy tabor?

Clown. No, sir, I live by the church.

Viola. Art thou a churchman?

Clown. No such matter, sir: I do live by the church; for I do live at my house, and my house doth stand by the church.

Viola. So thou mayst say, the king lies by a beggar, 10 if a beggar dwell near him; or, the church stands by thy tabor, if thy tabor stand by the church.

Clown. You have said, sir.—To see this age!—A sentence is but a cheveril glove to a good wit: how quickly the wrong side may be turned outward!

Viola. Nay, that's certain; they that dally nicely with words may quickly make them wanton.

Clown. I would, therefore, my sister had had no name, sir.   20

Viola. Why, man?

Clown. Why, sir, her name's a word. But indeed words are very rascals since bonds disgraced them.

Viola. Thy reason, man?

Clown. Troth, sir, I can yield you none without words; and words are grown so false, I am loth to prove reason with them.

Viola. I warrant thou art a merry fellow and carest 30 for nothing.

Clown. Not so, sir; I do care for something; but in my conscience, sir, I do not care for you: if that be to care for nothing, sir, I would it would make you invisible.

Viola. Art not thou the Lady Olivia's fool?

Clown. No, indeed, sir; the Lady Olivia has no folly: she will keep no fool, sir, till she be married; and fools are as like husbands as pilchards are to herrings,—the 40 husband's the bigger: I am, indeed, not her fool, but her corrupter of words.

Viola. I saw thee late at the Count Orsino's.

Clown. Foolery, sir, does walk about the orb like the sun, it shines everywhere. I would be sorry, sir, but the fool should be as oft with your master as with my mistress: I think I saw your wisdom there.

Viola. Nay, an thou pass upon me, I'll no more with thee. Hold, there's expenses for thee.

Clown. Now, Jove, in his next commodity of hair, 50 send thee a beard!

Viola. By my troth, I'll tell thee, I am almost sick for one; [*Aside*] though I would not have it grow on my chin. Is thy lady within?

Clown. Would not a pair of these have bred, sir?

Viola. Yes, being put to use.

Clown. I would play Lord Pandarus of Phrygia, sir, to bring a Cressida to this Troilus.

Viola. I understand you, sir; 'tis well begged.   60

Clown. The matter, I hope, is not great, sir, begging
but a beggar: Cressida was a beggar. My lady is within,
sir. I will construe to them whence you come; who you
are, and what you would, are out of my welkin,—I might
say element, but the word is over-worn.   [*Exit.*

Viola. This fellow's wise enough to play the fool;
And to do that well craves a kind of wit:
He must observe their mood on whom he jests,
70 The quality of persons, and the time;
And, like the haggard, check at every feather
That comes before his eye. This is a practice
As full of labour as a wise man's art:
For folly that he wisely shows is fit;
But wise men, folly-fall'n, quite taint their wit.

Enter Sir TOBY *and* Sir ANDREW.

Sir Toby. Save you, gentleman!
Viola. And you, sir.
Sir Andrew. Dieu vous garde, monsieur.
Viola. Et vous aussi; votre serviteur.
80   *Sir Andrew.* I hope, sir, you are; and I am yours.
Sir Toby. Will you encounter the house? my niece is
desirous you should enter, if your trade be to her.
Viola. I am bound to your niece, sir; I mean, she is
the list of my voyage.
Sir Toby. Taste your legs, sir; put them to motion.
Viola. My legs do better understand me, sir, than I
90 understand what you mean by bidding me taste my legs.
Sir Toby. I mean; to go, sir, to enter.
Viola. I will answer you with gait and entrance:—but
we are prevented.

Enter OLIVIA *and* MARIA.

Most excellent accomplished lady, the heavens rain odours
on you!
Sir Andrew. That youth's a rare courtier: "Rain
odours:"—well!

Viola. My matter hath no voice, lady, but to your
own most pregnant and vouchsafed ear.   100

Sir Andrew. "Odours," "pregnant," and "vouchsafed:"—I'll get 'em all three all ready.

Olivia. Let the garden-door be shut, and leave me to
my hearing. [*Exeunt Sir Toby, Sir Andrew, and Maria.*]
Give me your hand, sir.

Viola. My duty, madam, and most humble service.

Olivia. What is your name?

Viola. Cesario is your servant's name, fair princess.

Olivia. My servant, sir! 'Twas never merry world
Since lowly feigning was call'd compliment: 110
You're servant to the Count Orsino, youth.

Viola. And he is yours, and his must needs be yours:
Your servant's servant is your servant, madam.

Olivia. For him, I think not on him: for his thoughts,
Would they were blanks, rather than fill'd with me!

Viola. Madam, I come to whet your gentle thoughts
On his behalf:—

Olivia.   O, by your leave, I pray you;
I bade you never speak again of him:
But, would you undertake another suit,
I had rather hear you to solicit that   120
Than music from the spheres.

Viola.   Dear lady,—

Olivia. Give me leave, beseech you. I did send,
After the last enchantment you did here,
A ring in chase of you: so did I abuse
Myself, my servant, and, I fear me, you;
Under your hard construction must I sit,
To force that on you, in a shameful cunning,
Which you knew none of yours: what might you think?
Have you not set mine honour at the stake,
And baited it with all th' unmuzzled thoughts   130
That tyrannous heart can think? To one of your receiving
Enough is shown: a cyprus, not a bosom,
Hides my heart. So, let me hear you speak.

Viola. I pity you.

Olivia. That's a degree to love.

Viola. No, not a grize; for 'tis a vulgar proof,
That very oft we pity enemies.

Olivia. Why, then, methinks 'tis time to smile
again.
O world, how apt the poor are to be proud!
If one should be a prey, how much the better
140 To fall before the lion than the wolf!   [*Clock strikes.*
The clock upbraids me with the waste of time.
Be not afraid, good youth, I will not have you:
And yet, when wit and youth is come to harvest,
Your wife is like to reap a proper man:
There lies your way, due west.

Viola. Then westward-ho!
Grace and good disposition attend your ladyship!
You'll nothing, madam, to my lord by me?

Olivia. Stay:
150 I prithee, tell me what thou think'st of me.

Viola. That you do think you are not what you are.

Olivia. If I think so, I think the same of you.

Viola. Then think you right: I am not what I am.

Olivia. I would you were as I would have you be!

Viola. Would it be better, madam, than I am?
I wish it might, for now I am your fool.

Olivia. O what a deal of scorn looks beautiful
In the contempt and anger of his lip!
A murderous guilt shows not itself more soon
160 Than love that would seem hid: love's night is noon.
Cesario, by the roses of the spring,
By maidhood, honour, truth, and every thing,
I love thee so, that, maugre all thy pride,
Nor wit nor reason can my passion hide.
Do not extort thy reasons from this clause,
For that I woo, thou therefore hast no cause;
But, rather, reason thus with reason fetter,—
Love sought is good, but given unsought is better.

Viola. By innocence I swear, and by my youth,
I have one heart, one bosom, and one truth,   170
And that no woman has; nor never none
Shall mistress be of it, save I alone.
And so adieu, good madam: never more
Will I my master's tears to you deplore.
Olivia. Yet come again; for thou perhaps mayst move
That heart, which now abhors, to like his love. [*Exeunt.*

SCENE II. OLIVIA'S *house.*

Enter Sir TOBY, Sir ANDREW, *and* FABIAN.

Sir Andrew. No, faith, I'll not stay a jot longer.

Sir Toby. Thy reason, dear venom; give thy reason.

Fabian. You must needs yield your reason, Sir Andrew.

Sir Andrew. Marry, I saw your niece do more favours
to the count's serving-man than ever she bestowed upon
me; I saw't i' the orchard.

Sir Toby. Did she see thee the while, old boy? tell
me that.   10

Sir Andrew. As plain as I see you now.

Fabian. This was a great argument of love in her
toward you.

Sir Andrew. 'Slight, will you make an ass o' me?

Fabian. I will prove it legitimate, sir, upon the oaths
of judgment and reason.

Sir Toby. And they have been grand-jurymen since
before Noah was a sailor.

Fabian. She did show favour to the youth in your
sight only to exasperate you, to awake your dormouse 20
valour, to put fire in your heart, and brimstone in your
liver. You should then have accosted her; and with
some excellent jests, fire-new from the mint, you should
have banged the youth into dumbness. This was looked
for at your hand, and this was balked: the double gilt
of this opportunity you let time wash off, and you are
now sailed into the north of my lady's opinion; where

you will hang like an icicle on a Dutchman's beard,
30 unless you do redeem it by some laudable attempt either
of valour or policy.

Sir Andrew. An't be any way, it must be with
valour; for policy I hate: I had as lief be a Brownist as a
politician.

Sir Toby. Why, then, build me thy fortunes upon the
basis of valour. Challenge me the count's youth to fight
with him; hurt him in eleven places: my niece shall
take note of it; and assure thyself, there is no love-broker
40 in the world can more prevail in man's commendation
with woman than report of valour.

Fabian. There is no way but this, Sir Andrew.

Sir Andrew. Will either of you bear me a challenge
to him?

Sir Toby. Go, write it in a martial hand; be curst and
brief; it is no matter how witty, so it be eloquent and
full of invention: taunt him with the licence of ink: if
thou "thou'st" him some thrice, it shall not be amiss;
50 and as many lies as will lie in thy sheet of paper, although
the sheet were big enough for the bed of Ware in England,
set 'em down: go, about it. Let there be gall enough in
thy ink; though thou write with a goose-pen, no matter:
about it.

Sir Andrew. Where shall I find you?

Sir Toby. We'll call thee at the *cubiculo*: go.

[*Exit Sir Andrew.*

Fabian. This is a dear manakin to you, Sir Toby.

Sir Toby. I have been dear to him, lad,—some two
thousand strong, or so.

60 *Fabian.* We shall have a rare letter from him: but
you'll not deliver't?

Sir Toby. Never trust me, then; and by all means stir
on the youth to an answer. I think oxen and wainropes
cannot hale them together. For Andrew, if he were
opened, and you find so much blood in his liver as will
clog the foot of a flea, I'll eat the rest of the anatomy.

Fabian. And his opposite, the youth, bears in his visage no great presage of cruelty.

Sir Toby. Look, where the youngest wren of nine 70 comes.

Enter MARIA.

Maria. If you desire the spleen, and will laugh your-selves into stitches, follow me. Yond gull Malvolio is turned heathen, a very renegado; for there is no Christian, that means to be saved by believing rightly, can ever believe such impossible passages of grossness. He's in yellow stockings.

Sir Toby. And cross-gartered?

Maria. Most villanously; like a pedant that keeps a 80 school i' the church. I have dogged him, like his mur-derer. He does obey every point of the letter that I dropped to betray him: he does smile his face into more lines than are in the new map with the augmentation of the Indies: you have not seen such a thing as 'tis; I can hardly forbear hurling things at him. I know my lady will strike him: if she do, he'll smile, and take't for a great favour.

Sir Toby. Come, bring us, bring us where he is.   90

                                        [*Exeunt.*

SCENE III. *A street.*

Enter SEBASTIAN *and* ANTONIO.

Sebastian. I would not by my will have troubled you;
But, since you make your pleasure of your pains,
I will no further chide you.

Antonio. I could not stay behind you: my desire,
More sharp than filed steel, did spur me forth;
And not all love to see you,—though so much
As might have drawn one to a longer voyage,—
But jealousy what might befall your travel,
Being skilless in these parts; which to a stranger,
Unguided and unfriended, often prove   10

Rough and unhospitable: my willing love,
The rather by these arguments of fear,
Set forth in your pursuit.
    Sebastian.   My kind Antonio,
I can no other answer make, but thanks,
And thanks, and ever thanks; and oft good turns
Are shuffled off with such uncurrent pay:
But, were my worth as is my conscience firm,
You should find better dealing. What's to do?
Shall we go see the reliques of this town?
20   *Antonio.* To-morrow, sir; best first go see your lodging.
    Sebastian. I am not weary, and 'tis long to night:
I pray you, let us satisfy our eyes
With the memorials and the things of fame
That do renown this city.   •
    Antonio.   Would you'd pardon me;
I do not without danger walk these streets:
Once, in a sea-fight, 'gainst the count his galleys
I did some service; of such note, indeed,
That were I ta'en here it would scarce be answer'd.
    Sebastian. Belike you slew great number of his people?
30   *Antonio.* The offence is not of such a bloody nature;
Albeit the quality of the time and quarrel
Might well have given us bloody argument.
It might have since been answer'd in repaying
What we took from them; which, for traffic's sake,
Most of our city did: only myself stood out;
For which, if I be lapsed in this place,
I shall pay dear.
    Sebastian.   Do not, then, walk too often.
    Antonio. It doth not fit me. Hold, sir, here's my
        purse.
In the south suburbs, at the Elephant,
40 Is best to lodge: I will bespeak our diet,
Whiles you beguile the time and feed your knowledge
With viewing of the town: there shall you have me.
    Sebastian. Why I your purse?

Antonio. Haply your eye shall light upon some toy
You have desire to purchase; and your store,
I think, is not for idle markets, sir.

Sebastian. I'll be your purse-bearer and leave you
For an hour.

Antonio. To the Elephant.

Sebastian.   I do remember. [*Exeunt.*

Scene IV. Olivia's *garden.*

Enter Olivia *and* Maria.

Olivia. I have sent after him: he says he'll come;—
How shall I feast him? what bestow of him?
For youth is bought more oft than begg'd or borrow'd.
I speak too loud.—
Where is Malvolio?—he is sad and civil,
And suits well for a servant with my fortunes:—
Where is Malvolio?

Maria. He's coming, madam; but in very strange
manner. He is, sure, possessed, madam.

Olivia. Why, what's the matter? does he rave?   10

Maria. No, madam, he does nothing but smile: your
ladyship were best to have some guard about you, if he
come; for, sure, the man is tainted in's wits.

Olivia. Go call him hither. [*Exit Maria.*] I'm as mad
        as he,
If sad and merry madness equal be.

Re-enter Maria, *with* Malvolio.

How now, Malvolio!

Malvolio. Sweet lady, ho ho.

Olivia. Smilest thou?
I sent for thee upon a sad occasion.   20

Malvolio. Sad, lady! I could be sad: this does make
some obstruction in the blood, this cross-gartering;
but what of that? if it please the eye of one, it is

with me as the very true sonnet is, "Please one, and please all."

Olivia. Why, how dost thou, man? what is the matter with thee?

Malvolio. Not black in my mind, though yellow in my legs. It did come to his hands, and commands 30 shall be executed: I think we do know the sweet Roman hand.

Olivia. Wilt thou go to bed, Malvolio?

Malvolio. To bed!

Olivia. God comfort thee! Why dost thou smile so and kiss thy hand so oft?

Maria. How do you, Malvolio?

Malvolio. At your request! yes; nightingales answer daws.

40 *Maria.* Why appear you with this ridiculous boldness before my lady?

Malvolio. "Be not afraid of greatness:"—'twas well writ.

Olivia. What meanest thou by that, Malvolio?

Malvolio. "Some are born great,"—

Olivia. Ha!

Malvolio. "Some achieve greatness,"—

Olivia. What sayest thou?

Malvolio. "And some have greatness thrust upon 50 them."

Olivia. Heaven restore thee!

Malvolio. "Remember who commended thy yellow stockings,"—

Olivia. Thy yellow stockings!

Malvolio. "And wished to see thee cross-gartered."

Olivia. Cross-gartered!

Malvolio. "Go to, thou art made, if thou desirest to be so;"—

Olivia. Am I made?

60 *Malvolio.* "If not, let me see thee a servant still."

Olivia. Why, this is very midsummer madness.

Enter Servant.

Servant. Madam, the young gentleman of the Count
Orsino's is returned: I could hardly entreat him back:
he attends your ladyship's pleasure.

Olivia. I'll come to him. [*Exit Servant.*] Good
Maria, let this fellow be looked to. Where's my cousin
Toby? Let some of my people have a special care of
him: I would not have him miscarry for the half of my
dowry.   [*Exeunt Olivia and Maria.* 70

Malvolio. O, ho! do you come near me now? no
worse man than Sir Toby to look to me? This concurs
directly with the letter: she sends him on purpose, that
I may appear stubborn to him; for she incites me to
that in the letter. "Cast thy humble slough," says she;
"be opposite with a kinsman, surly with servants; let
thy tongue tang with arguments of state; put thyself into
the trick of singularity;"—and, consequently, sets down 80
the manner how; as, a sad face, a reverent carriage, a
slow tongue, in the habit of some sir of note, and so
forth. I have limed her; but it is Jove's doing, and Jove
make me thankful! And, when she went away now,
"Let this fellow be looked to:" fellow! not Malvolio,
nor after my degree, but fellow. Why, everything adheres
together, that no dram of a scruple, no scruple of a
scruple, no obstacle, no incredulous or unsafe circumstance—What can be said? Nothing that can be can 90
come between me and the full prospect of my hopes.
Well, Jove, not I, is the doer of this, and he is to be
thanked.

Re-enter MARIA, *with* Sir TOBY *and* FABIAN.

Sir Toby. Which way is he, in the name of sanctity?
If all the devils of hell be drawn in little, and Legion
himself possessed him, yet I'll speak to him.

Fabian. Here he is, here he is.—How is't with you,
sir? how is't with you, man?

Malvolio. Go off; I discard you: let me enjoy my
100 private: go off.

Maria. Lo, how hollow the fiend speaks within him!
did not I tell you?—Sir Toby, my lady prays you to
have a care of him.

Malvolio. Ah, ah! does she so?

Sir Toby. Go to, go to; peace, peace; we must deal
gently with him: let me alone.—How do you, Malvolio?
how is't with you? What, man! defy the devil: consider,
he's an enemy to mankind.

110   *Malvolio.* Do you know what you say?

Maria. La you, an you speak ill of the devil, how he
takes it at heart! Pray God, he be not bewitched! My
lady would not lose him for more than I'll say.

Malvolio. How now, mistress!

Maria. O Lord!

120   *Sir Toby.* Prithee, hold thy peace; this is not the way:
do you not see you move him? let me alone with him.

Fabian. No way but gentleness; gently, gently: the
fiend is rough, and will not be roughly used.

Sir Toby. Why, how now, my bawcock! how dost
thou, chuck?

Malvolio. Sir!

Sir Toby. Ay, Biddy, come with me. What, man!
'tis not for gravity to play at cherry-pit with Satan: hang
130 him, foul collier!

Maria. Get him to say his prayers; good Sir Toby,
get him to pray.

Malvolio. My prayers, minx!

Maria. No, I warrant you, he will not hear of godli-
ness.

Malvolio. Go, hang yourselves all! you are idle shallow
things: I am not of your element: you shall know more
hereafter.   [*Exit.*

Sir Toby. Is't possible?

140   *Fabian.* If this were played upon a stage now, I could
condemn it as an improbable fiction.

Sir Toby. His very genius hath taken the infection of the device, man.

Maria. Nay, pursue him now, lest the device take air and taint.

Fabian. Why, we shall make him mad indeed.

Maria. The house will be the quieter.

Sir Toby. Come, we'll have him in a dark room and bound. My niece is already in the belief that he's mad; 150 we may carry it thus, for our pleasure and his penance, till our very pastime, tired out of breath, prompt us to have mercy on him: at which time we will bring the device to the bar, and crown thee for a finder of madmen.—But see, but see.

Fabian. More matter for a May morning.

Enter Sir ANDREW.

Sir Andrew. Here's the challenge, read it: I warrant there's vinegar and pepper in't.

Fabian. Is't so saucy?

Sir Andrew. Ay, is't, I warrant him: do but read. 160

Sir Toby. Give me. [*Reads*] "Youth, whatsoever thou art, thou art but a scurvy fellow."

Fabian. Good, and valiant.

Sir Toby. [*Reads*] "Wonder not, nor admire not in thy mind, why I do call thee so, for I will show thee no reason for't."

Fabian. A good note: that keeps you from the blow of the law.

Sir Toby. [*Reads*] "Thou comest to the Lady Olivia, 170 and in my sight she uses thee kindly: but thou liest in thy throat; that is not the matter I challenge thee for."

Fabian. Very brief, and to exceeding good sense—less.

Sir Toby. [*Reads*] "I will waylay thee going home; where if it be thy chance to kill me,"—

Fabian. Good.

Sir Toby. [*Reads*] "Thou killest me like a rogue and a villain." 180

Fabian. Still you keep o' the windy side of the law: good.

Sir Toby. [*Reads*] "Fare thee well; and God have mercy upon one of our souls! He may have mercy upon mine; but my hope is better, and so look to thyself. Thy friend, as thou usest him, and thy sworn enemy,

ANDREW AGUECHEEK."

If this letter move him not, his legs cannot: I'll give't him.

190 *Maria.* You may have very fit occasion for't: he is now in some commerce with my lady, and will by and by depart.

Sir Toby. Go, Sir Andrew; scout me for him at the corner of the orchard, like a bum-baily: so soon as ever thou seest him, draw; and, as thou drawest, swear horrible; for it comes to pass oft that a terrible oath, with a swaggering accent sharply twanged off, gives manhood more approbation than ever proof itself would have

200 earned him. Away!

Sir Andrew. Nay, let me alone for swearing.   [*Exit.*

Sir Toby. Now will not I deliver his letter: for the behaviour of the young gentleman gives him out to be of good capacity and breeding; his employment between his lord and my niece confirms no less: therefore this letter, being so excellently ignorant, will breed no terror in the youth,—he will find it comes from a clodpole. But, sir, I will deliver his challenge by word of mouth;

210 set upon Aguecheek a notable report of valour; and drive the gentleman—as I know his youth will aptly receive it—into a most hideous opinion of his rage, skill, fury, and impetuosity. This will so fright them both, that they will kill one another by the look, like cockatrices.

Fabian. Here he comes with your niece: give them way till he take leave, and presently after him.

Sir Toby. I will meditate the while upon some horrid

220 message for a challenge.

[*Exeunt Sir Toby, Fabian, and Maria.*

Re-enter OLIVIA, *with* VIOLA.

Olivia. I have said too much unto a heart of stone,
And laid mine honour too unchary on't:
There's something in me that reproves my fault;
But such a headstrong potent fault it is,
That it but mocks reproof.

Viola. With the same 'haviour that your passion bears
Goes on my master's grief.

Olivia. Here, wear this jewel for me, 'tis my picture:
Refuse it not; it hath no tongue to vex you:
And I beseech you come again to-morrow.   230
What shall you ask of me that I'll deny,
That honour sav'd may upon asking give?

Viola. Nothing but this,—your true love for my master.

Olivia. How with mine honour may I give him that
Which I have given to you?

Viola.   I will acquit you.

Olivia. Well, come again to-morrow: fare thee well:
A fiend like thee might bear my soul to hell.   [*Exit*.

Re-enter Sir TOBY *and* FABIAN.

Sir Toby. Gentleman, God save thee!

Viola. And you, sir.

Sir Toby. That defence thou hast, betake thee to't: 240
of what nature the wrongs are thou hast done him, I
know not; but thy intercepter, full of despite, bloody as
the hunter, attends thee at the orchard-end: dismount
thy tuck, be yare in thy preparation; for thy assailant is
quick, skilful, and deadly.

Viola. You mistake, sir; I am sure no man hath any
quarrel to me: my remembrance is very free and clear
from any image of offence done to any man.   250

Sir Toby. You'll find it otherwise, I assure you:
therefore, if you hold your life at any price, betake you
to your guard; for your opposite hath in him what
youth, strength, skill, and wrath can furnish man withal.

Viola. I pray you, sir, what is he?

Sir Toby. He is knight, dubbed with unhatched rapier
and on carpet consideration; but he is a devil in private
260 brawl: souls and bodies hath he divorced three; and his
incensement at this moment is so implacable, that satisfaction can be none but by pangs of death and sepulchre:
hob, nob, is his word; give't or take't.

Viola. I will return again into the house and desire
some conduct of the lady. I am no fighter. I have heard
of some kind of men that put quarrels purposely on others,
to taste their valour: belike this is a man of that quirk.

Sir Toby. Sir, no; his indignation derives itself out
270 of a very competent injury: therefore, get you on and
give him his desire. Back you shall not to the house,
unless you undertake that with me which with as much
safety you might answer him: therefore, on, or strip
your sword stark naked; for meddle you must, that's
certain, or forswear to wear iron about you.

Viola. This is as uncivil as strange. I beseech you,
do me this courteous office, as to know of the knight
what my offence to him is: it is something of my negli-
280 gence, nothing of my purpose.

Sir Toby. I will do so.—Signior Fabian, stay you by
this gentleman till my return.   [*Exit.*

Viola. Pray you, sir, do you know of this matter?

Fabian. I know the knight is incensed against you,
even to a mortal arbitrement; but nothing of the circumstance more.

Viola. I beseech you, what manner of man is he?

290 *Fabian.* Nothing of that wonderful promise, to read
him by his form, as you are like to find him in the
proof of his valour. He is, indeed, sir, the most skilful,
bloody, and fatal opposite that you could possibly have
found in any part of Illyria. Will you walk towards him?
I will make your peace with him, if I can.

Viola. I shall be much bound to you for't: I am one
that had rather go with sir priest than sir knight: I care
300 not who knows so much of my mettle.   [*Exeunt.*

Re-enter Sir TOBY, *with* Sir ANDREW.

Sir Toby. Why, man, he's a very devil; I have not
seen such a firago. I had a pass with him, rapier,
scabbard, and all, and he gives me the stuck in with
such a mortal motion, that it is inevitable; and on
the answer, he pays you as surely as your feet hit the
ground they step on: they say he has been fencer to the
Sophy.

Sir Andrew. I'll not meddle with him.

Sir Toby. Ay, but he will not now be pacified: Fabian
can scarce hold him yonder.   310

Sir Andrew. Plague on't, an I thought he had been
valiant and so cunning in fence, I'd have seen him
damned ere I'd have challenged him. Let him let the
matter slip, and I'll give him my horse, gray Capilet.

Sir Toby. I'll make the motion: stand here, make a
good show on't: this shall end without the perdition of
souls.—[*Aside*] Marry, I'll ride your horse as well as I
ride you.

Re-enter FABIAN *and* VIOLA.

[*To Fabian*] I have his horse to take up the quarrel: I   320
have persuaded him the youth's a devil.

Fabian. He is as horribly conceited of him; and pants
and looks pale, as if a bear were at his heels.

Sir Toby. [*To Viola*] There's no remedy, sir; he will
fight with you for's oath sake: marry, he hath better
bethought him of his quarrel, and he finds that now
scarce to be worth talking of: therefore draw, for the
supportance of his vow; he protests he will not hurt
you.   330

Viola. [*Aside*] Pray God defend me! A little thing
would make me tell them how much I lack of a man.

Fabian. Give ground, if you see him furious.

Sir Toby. Come, Sir Andrew, there's no remedy; the
gentleman will, for his honour's sake, have one bout with
you; he cannot by the duello avoid it: but he has promised

me, as he is a gentleman and a soldier, he will not hurt
340 you. Come on; to't.

 Sir Andrew. Pray God he keep his oath! [*Draws.*

 Viola. I do assure you, 'tis against my will. [*Draws.*

Enter ANTONIO.

 Antonio. Put up your sword. If this young gentleman
Have done offence, I take the fault on me:
If you offend him, I for him defy you.

 Sir Toby. You, sir! why, what are you?

 Antonio. One, sir, that for his love dares yet do more
Than you have heard him brag to you he will. [*Draws.*

 Sir Toby. Nay, if you be an undertaker, I am for
350 you. [*Draws.*

 Fabian. O good Sir Toby, hold! here come the officers.

 Sir Toby. [*To Antonio*] I'll be with you anon.

 Viola. [*To Sir Andrew*] Pray, sir, put your sword up,
if you please.

 Sir Andrew. Marry, will I, sir; and, for that I promised
you, I'll be as good as my word: he will bear you easily and
reins well.

Enter Officers.

 First Officer. This is the man; do thy office.

360 *Second Officer.* Antonio, I arrest thee at the suit
Of Count Orsino.

 Antonio.   You do mistake me, sir.

 First Officer. No, sir, no jot; I know your favour well,
Though now you have no sea-cap on your head.—
Take him away: he knows I know him well.

 Antonio. I must obey.—[*To Viola*] This comes with
seeking you:
But there's no remedy; I shall answer it.
What will you do, now my necessity
Makes me to ask you for my purse? It grieves me
370 Much more for what I cannot do for you
Than what befalls myself. You stand amaz'd;
But be of comfort.

Second Officer. Come, sir, away.

Antonio. I must entreat of you some of that money.

Viola. What money, sir?

For the fair kindness you have show'd me here,
And, part, being prompted by your present trouble,
Out of my lean and low ability
I'll lend you something: my having is not much;
I'll make division of my present with you: 380
Hold, there's half my coffer.

Antonio.   Will you deny me now?
Is't possible that my deserts to you
Can lack persuasion? Do not tempt my misery,
Lest that it make me so unsound a man
As to upbraid you with those kindnesses
That I have done for you.

Viola.   I know of none;
Nor know I you by voice or any feature:
I hate ingratitude more in a man
Than lying, vainness, babbling, drunkenness,
Or any taint of vice whose strong corruption   390
Inhabits our frail blood.

Antonio.   O heavens themselves!

Second Officer. Come, sir, I pray you, go.

Antonio. Let me speak a little. This youth that you
          see here
I snatch'd one half out of the jaws of death;
Reliev'd him with such sanctity of love,
And to his image, which methought did promise
Most venerable worth, did I devotion.

First Officer. What's that to us? The time goes by:
          away!

Antonio. But O how vile an idol proves this god!
Thou hast, Sebastian, done good feature shame.   400
In nature there's no blemish but the mind:
None can be call'd deform'd but the unkind:
Virtue is beauty; but the beauteous-evil
Are empty trunks, o'erflourish'd by the devil.

First Officer. The man grows mad: away with him!—
Come, come, sir.

Antonio. Lead me on.   [*Exeunt Officers with Antonio.*

Viola. Methinks his words do from such passion fly,
That he believes himself: so do not I.
Prove true, imagination, O prove true,
410 That I, dear brother, be now ta'en for you!

Sir Toby. Come hither, knight; come hither, Fabian:
we'll whisper o'er a couplet or two of most sage saws.

Viola. He nam'd Sebastian: I my brother know
Yet living in my glass; even such and so
In favour was my brother; and he went
Still in this fashion, colour, ornament,—
For him I imitate: O, if it prove,
Tempests are kind, and salt waves fresh in love!   [*Exit.*

420 *Sir Toby.* A very dishonest paltry boy, and more a
coward than a hare: his dishonesty appears in leaving
his friend here in necessity and denying him; and for
his cowardship, ask Fabian.

Fabian. A coward, a most devout coward, religious in it.

Sir Andrew. 'Slid, I'll after him again, and beat him.

Sir Toby. Do; cuff him soundly, but never draw thy
sword.

430 *Sir Andrew.* An I do not,—   [*Exit.*

Fabian. Come, let's see the event.

Sir Toby. I dare lay any money 'twill be nothing yet.
        [*Exeunt.*

ACT IV.

Scene I. *Before* Olivia's *house.*

Enter Sebastian *and* Clown.

Clown. Will you make me believe that I am not sent
for you?

Sebastian. Go to, go to, thou art a foolish fellow:
Let me be clear of thee.

Clown. Well held out, i' faith! No, I do not know you; nor I am not sent to you by my lady, to bid you come speak with her; nor your name is not Master Cesario; nor this is not my nose neither. Nothing that is so is so.

Sebastian. I prithee, vent thy folly somewhere else: 10
Thou know'st not me.

Clown. Vent my folly! he has heard that word of some great man, and now applies it to a fool: vent my folly! I am afraid this great lubber, the world, will prove a cockney.—I prithee, now, ungird thy strangeness, and tell me what I shall vent to my lady: shall I vent to her that thou art coming?

Sebastian. I prithee, foolish Greek, depart from me:
There's money for thee: if you tarry longer, 20
I shall give worse payment.

Clown. By my troth, thou hast an open hand. These wise men, that give fools money, get themselves a good report—after fourteen years' purchase.

Enter Sir ANDREW, Sir TOBY, *and* FABIAN.

Sir Andrew. Now, sir, have I met you again? there's
for you. [*Striking Sebastian.*

Sebastian. Why, there's for thee, and there, and there!
[*Beating Sir Andrew.*
Are all the people mad?

Sir Toby. Hold, sir, or I'll throw your dagger o'er 30
the house.

Clown. This will I tell my lady straight: I would not
be in some of your coats for twopence. [*Exit.*

Sir Toby. Come on, sir; hold.

Sir Andrew. Nay, let him alone: I'll go another way
to work with him; I'll have an action of battery against
him, if there be any law in Illyria: though I struck him
first, yet it's no matter for that.

Sebastian. Let go thy hand. 40

Sir Toby. Come, sir, I will not let you go. Come, my

young soldier, put up your iron: you are well fleshed;
come on.

    Sebastian. I will be free from thee. [*Disengages him-
        self.*] What wouldst thou now?
If thou dar'st tempt me further, draw thy sword. [*Draws.*
    Sir Toby. What, what? Nay, then I must have an
ounce or two of this malapert blood from you.   [*Draws.*

                 Enter OLIVIA.

    Olivia. Hold, Toby; on thy life, I charge thee, hold!
50   *Sir Toby.* Madam!
    Olivia. Will it be ever thus? Ungracious wretch,
Fit for the mountains and the barbarous caves,
Where manners ne'er were preach'd! out of my sight!—
Be not offended, dear Cesario.—
Rudesby, be gone!
        [*Exeunt Sir Toby, Sir Andrew, and Fabian.*
                I prithee, gentle friend,
Let thy fair wisdom, not thy passion, sway
In this uncivil and unjust extent
Against thy peace. Go with me to my house;
And hear thou there how many fruitless pranks
60 This ruffian hath botch'd up, that thou thereby
Mayst smile at this: thou shalt not choose but go:
Do not deny. Beshrew his soul for me,
He started one poor heart of mine in thee.
    Sebastian. What relish is in this? how runs the
        stream?
Or I am mad, or else this is a dream:
Let fancy still my sense in Lethe steep;
If it be thus to dream, still let me sleep!
    Olivia. Nay, come, I prithee: would thou'dst be rul'd
        by me!
    Sebastian. Madam, I will.
    Olivia.   O, say so, and so be!
                      [*Exeunt.*

SCENE II. OLIVIA's *house*.

Enter MARIA *and* Clown.

Maria. Nay, I prithee, put on this gown and this beard; make him believe thou art Sir Topas the curate: do it quickly; I'll call Sir Toby the whilst.   [*Exit.*

Clown. Well, I'll put it on, and I will dissemble myself in't; and I would I were the first that ever dissembled in such a gown. I am not tall enough to become the function well, nor lean enough to be thought a good student: but to be said an honest man and a good house- 10 keeper goes as fairly as to say a careful man and a great scholar. The competitors enter.

Enter Sir TOBY *and* MARIA.

Sir Toby. Jove bless thee, master parson.

Clown. Bonos dies, Sir Toby: for, as the old hermit of Prague, that never saw pen and ink, very wittily said to a niece of King Gorboduc, "That that is is;" so I, being master parson, am master parson; for, what is that but that, and is but is?

Sir Toby. To him, Sir Topas.   20

Clown. What, ho, I say! peace in this prison!

Sir Toby. The knave counterfeits well; a good knave.

Malvolio. [*Within*] Who calls there?

Clown. Sir Topas the curate, who comes to visit Malvolio the lunatic.

Malvolio. Sir Topas, Sir Topas, good Sir Topas, go to my lady.

Clown. Out, hyperbolical fiend! how vexest thou this man! talkest thou nothing but of ladies?   30

Sir Toby. Well said, master parson.

Malvolio. Sir Topas, never was man thus wronged: good Sir Topas, do not think I am mad: they have laid me here in hideous darkness.

Clown. Fie, thou dishonest Satan! I call thee by the most modest terms; for I am one of those gentle ones that will use the devil himself with courtesy: sayest thou that house is dark?

Malvolio. As hell, Sir Topas.

40 *Clown.* Why, it hath bay-windows transparent as barricadoes, and the clear-stories toward the south-north are as lustrous as ebony; and yet complainest thou of obstruction?

Malvolio. I am not mad, Sir Topas: I say to you, this house is dark.

Clown. Madman, thou errest: I say, there is no darkness but ignorance; in which thou art more puzzled than the Egyptians in their fog.

Malvolio. I say, this house is as dark as ignorance, 50 though ignorance were as dark as hell; and I say, there was never man thus abused. I am no more mad than you are: make the trial of it in any constant question.

Clown. What is the opinion of Pythagoras concerning wildfowl?

Malvolio. That the soul of our grandam might haply inhabit a bird.

Clown. What thinkest thou of his opinion?

Malvolio. I think nobly of the soul, and no way ap-60 prove his opinion.

Clown. Fare thee well. Remain thou still in darkness: thou shalt hold the opinion of Pythagoras ere I will allow of thy wits; and fear to kill a woodcock, lest thou dispossess the soul of thy grandam. Fare thee well.

Malvolio. Sir Topas, Sir Topas!

Sir Toby. My most exquisite Sir Topas!

Clown. Nay, I am for all waters.

Maria. Thou mightst have done this without thy 70 beard and gown: he sees thee not.

Sir Toby. To him in thine own voice, and bring me

word how thou findest him: I would we were well rid
of this knavery. If he may be conveniently delivered, I
would he were; for I am now so far in offence with my
niece that I cannot pursue with any safety this sport to
the upshot. Come by and by to my chamber.

                            [Exeunt Sir Toby and Maria.

  Clown. [*Singing*] "Hey, Robin, jolly Robin,

                 Tell me how thy lady does."

  Malvolio. Fool!   80

  Clown. "My lady is unkind, perdy."

  Malvolio. Fool!

  Clown. "Alas, why is she so?"

  Malvolio. Fool, I say!

  Clown. "She loves another"—Who calls, ha?

  Malvolio. Good fool, as ever thou wilt deserve well at
my hand, help me to a candle, and pen, ink, and paper:
as I am a gentleman, I will live to be thankful to thee
for't.

  Clown. Master Malvolio?   90

  Malvolio. Ay, good fool.

  Clown. Alas, sir, how fell you besides your five wits?

  Malvolio. Fool, there was never man so notoriously
abused: I am as well in my wits, fool, as thou art.

  Clown. But as well? then you are mad indeed, if you
be no better in your wits than a fool.

  Malvolio. They have here propertied me; keep me in
darkness, send ministers to me, asses, and do all they 100
can to face me out of my wits.

  Clown. Advise you what you say; the minister is
here.—Malvolio, Malvolio, thy wits the heavens restore!
endeavour thyself to sleep, and leave thy vain bibble-
babble.

  Malvolio. Sir Topas!

  Clown. Maintain no words with him, good fellow.—
Who, I, sir? not I, sir. God be wi' you, good Sir Topas!
—Marry, amen.—I will, sir, I will.

  Malvolio. Fool, fool, fool, I say!   110

Clown. Alas, sir, be patient. What say you, sir? I am shent for speaking to you.

Malvolio. Good fool, help me to some light and some paper: I tell thee, I am as well in my wits as any man in Illyria.

Clown. Well-a-day that you were, sir!

Malvolio. By this hand, I am. Good fool, some ink, paper, and light; and convey what I will set down to my lady: it shall advantage thee more than ever the
120 bearing of letter did.

Clown. I will help you to't. But tell me true, are you not mad indeed? or do you but counterfeit?

Malvolio. Believe me, I am not; I tell thee true.

Clown. Nay, I'll ne'er believe a madman till I see his brains. I will fetch you light, and paper, and ink.

Malvolio. Fool, I'll requite it in the highest degree: I prithee, be gone.

Clo. [*Singing*]

130   I am gone, sir,
                    And anon, sir,
                I'll be with you again,
                    In a trice,
                    Like to the old Vice, N. B.
                Your need to sustain;

                Who, with dagger of lath,
                In his rage and his wrath,
                    Cries, ah, ha! to the devil:
                Like a mad lad,
140   Pare thy nails, dad;
                    Adieu, goodman devil.   [*Exit.*

SCENE III. OLIVIA'S *garden.*

Enter SEBASTIAN.

Sebastian. This is the air; that is the glorious sun;
This pearl she gave me, I do feel't and see't:
And though 'tis wonder that enwraps me thus,

Yet 'tis not madness. Where's Antonio, then?
I could not find him at the Elephant:
Yet there he was; and there I found this credit,
That he did range the town to seek me out.
His counsel now might do me golden service;
For though my soul disputes well with my sense
That this may be some error, but no madness,   10
Yet doth this accident and flood of fortune
So far exceed all instance, all discourse,
That I am ready to distrust mine eyes,
And wrangle with my reason that persuades me
To any other trust but that I am mad,
Or else the lady's mad; yet, if 'twere so,
She could not sway her house, command her followers,
Take and give back affairs and their dispatch
With such a smooth, discreet, and stable bearing
As I perceive she does: there's something in't   20
That is deceivable. But here the lady comes.

Enter OLIVIA *and a* Priest.

Olivia. Blame not this haste of mine. If you **mean**
    well,
Now go with me and with this holy man
Into the chantry by: there, before him,
And underneath that consecrated roof,
Plight me the full assurance of your faith;
That my most jealous and too doubtful soul
May live at peace. He shall conceal it
Whiles you are willing it shall come to note,
What time we will our celebration keep   30
According to my birth.—What do you say?
Sebastian. I'll follow this good man, and go with you;
And, having sworn truth, ever will be true.
Olivia. Then lead the way, good father; and heavens
    so shine,
That they may fairly note this act of mine!   [*Exeunt.*

ACT V.

Scene I. *Before* Olivia's *house.*

Enter Clown *and* Fabian.

Fabian. Now, as thou lovest me, let me see his letter.

Clown. Good Master Fabian, grant me another request.

Fabian. Any thing.

Clown. Do not desire to see this letter.

Fabian. This is, to give a dog, and in recompense desire my dog again.

Enter Duke, Viola, Curio, *and* Lords.

Duke. Belong you to the Lady Olivia, friends?

10 *Clown.* Ay, sir; we are some of her trappings.

Duke. I know thee well: how dost thou, my good fellow?

Clown. Truly, sir, the better for my foes, and the worse for my friends.

Duke. Just the contrary; the better for thy friends.

Clown. No, sir, the worse.

Duke. How can that be?

Clown. Marry, sir, they praise me and make an ass of 20 me; now my foes tell me plainly I am an ass: so that by my foes, sir, I profit in the knowledge of myself, and by my friends I am abused: so that, conclusions to be as kisses, if your four negatives make your two affirmatives, why, then, the worse for my friends and the better for my foes.

Duke. Why, this is excellent.

Clown. By my troth, sir, no; though it please you to 30 be one of my friends.

Duke. Thou shalt not be the worse for me: there's gold.

Clown. But that it would be double-dealing, sir, I would you could make it another.

Duke. O, you give me ill counsel.

Clown. Put your grace in your pocket, sir, for this once, and let your flesh and blood obey it.

Duke. Well, I will be so much a sinner to be a double-dealer: there's another.

Clown. Primo, secundo, tertio, is a good play; and the old saying is, the third pays for all: the *triplex,* sir, is a 40 good tripping measure; or the bells of Saint Bennet, sir, may put you in mind,—one, two, three.

Duke. You can fool no more money out of me at this throw: if you will let your lady know I am here to speak with her, and bring her along with you, it may awake my bounty further.

Clown. Marry, sir, lullaby to your bounty till I come again. I go, sir; but I would not have you to think that my desire of having is the sin of covetousness: but, as 50 you say, sir, let your bounty take a nap, I will awake it anon.   [*Exit.*

Viola. Here comes the man, sir, that did rescue me.

Enter ANTONIO *and* Officers.

Duke. That face of his I do remember well;
Yet, when I saw it last, it was besmear'd
As black as Vulcan in the smoke of war:
A bawbling vessel was he captain of,
For shallow draught and bulk unprizable;
With which such scatheful grapple did he make
With the most noble bottom of our fleet,   60
That very envy and the tongue of loss
Cried fame and honour on him.—What's the matter?

First Officer. Orsino, this is that Antonio
That took the Phœnix and her fraught from Candy;
And this is he that did the Tiger board,
When your young nephew Titus lost his leg:
Here in the streets, desperate of shame and state,
In private brabble did we apprehend him.

Viola. He did me kindness, sir, drew on my side;
But in conclusion put strange speech upon me: 70

I know not what 'twas but distraction.

Duke. Notable pirate! thou salt-water thief!
What foolish boldness brought thee to their mercies,
Whom thou, in terms so bloody and so dear,
Hast made thine enemies?

Antonio.   Orsino, noble sir,
Be pleas'd that I shake off these names you give me:
Antonio never yet was thief or pirate,
Though, I confess, on base and ground enough,
Orsino's enemy. A witchcraft drew me hither:
80 That most ingrateful boy there by your side,
From the rude sea's enrag'd and foamy mouth
Did I redeem; a wreck past hope he was:
His life I gave him, and did thereto add
My love, without retention or restraint,
All his in dedication; for his sake
Did I expose myself, pure for his love,
Into the danger of this adverse town;
Drew to defend him when he was beset:
Where being apprehended, his false cunning—
90 Not meaning to partake with me in danger—
Taught him to face me out of his acquaintance,
And grew a twenty-years-removed thing
While one would wink; denied me mine own purse,
Which I had recommended to his use
Not half an hour before.

Viola.   How can this be?

Duke. When came he to this town?

Antonio. To-day, my lord: and for three months
    before,
No interim, not a minute's vacancy,
Both day and night did we keep company.

100 *Duke.* Here comes the countess: now heaven walks on
    earth.—
But for thee, fellow,—fellow, thy words are madness:
Three months this youth hath tended upon me;
But more of that anon.—Take him aside.

Enter OLIVIA *and* Attendants.

Olivia. What would my lord, but that he may not have,
Wherein Olivia may seem serviceable?—
Cesario, you do not keep promise with me.

Viola. Madam!

Duke. Gracious Olivia,—

Olivia. What do you say, Cesario?—Good my lord,—

Viola. My lord would speak; my duty hushes me.   110

Olivia. If it be aught to the old tune, my lord,
It is as fat and fulsome to mine ear
As howling after music.

Duke.   Still so cruel?

Olivia. Still so constant, lord.

Duke. What, to perverseness? you uncivil lady,
To whose ingrate and unauspicious altars
My soul the faithfull'st offerings hath breath'd out
That e'er devotion tender'd! What shall I do?

Olivia. Even what it please my lord, that shall become
          him.

Duke. Why should I not, had I the heart to do it,   120
Like to the Egyptian thief at point of death,
Kill what I love? a savage jealousy
That sometime savours nobly. But hear me this:
Since you to non-regardance cast my faith,
And that I partly know the instrument
That screws me from my true place in your favour,
Live you the marble-breasted tyrant still;
But this your minion, whom I know you love,
And whom, by heaven I swear, I tender dearly,
Him will I tear out of that cruel eye,   130
Where he sits crowned in his master's spite.
Come, boy, with me; my thoughts are ripe in mischief:
I'll sacrifice the lamb that I do love,
To spite a raven's heart within a dove.

Viola. And I, most jocund, apt and willingly,
To do you rest, a thousand deaths would die.

    Olivia. Where goes Cesario?
    Viola.   After him I love
More than I love these eyes, more than my life,
More, by all mores, than e'er I shall love wife.
140 If I do feign, you witnesses above
Punish my life for tainting of my love!
    Olivia. Ay me, detested! how am I beguil'd!
    Viola. Who does beguile you? who does do you wrong?
    Olivia. Hast thou forgot thyself? is it so long?
Call forth the holy father.
    Duke.   [*To Viola*] Come away!
    Olivia. Whither, my lord?—Cesario, husband, stay.
    Duke. Husband!
    Olivia.   Ay, husband: can he that deny?
    Duke. Her husband, sirrah!
    Viola.   No, my lord, not I.
    Olivia. Alas, it is the baseness of thy fear
150 That makes thee strangle thy propriety:
Fear not, Cesario; take thy fortunes up;
Be that thou know'st thou art, and then thou art
As great as that thou fear'st.

                    Enter Priest.

                O, welcome, father!
Father, I charge thee, by thy reverence,
Here to unfold—though lately we intended
To keep in darkness what occasion now
Reveals before 'tis ripe—what thou dost know
Hath newly pass'd between this youth and me.
    Priest. A contract of eternal bond of love,
160 Confirm'd by mutual joinder of your hands,
Attested by the holy close of lips,
Strengthen'd by interchangement of your rings;
And all the ceremony of this compact
Seal'd in my function, by my testimony:
Since when, my watch hath told me, toward my grave
I have travell'd but two hours.

Duke. O thou dissembling cub! what wilt thou be
When time hath sow'd a grizzle on thy case?
Or will not else thy craft so quickly grow,
That thine own trip shall be thine overthrow?   170
Farewell, and take her; but direct thy feet
Where thou and I henceforth may never meet.
    Viola. My lord, I do protest,—
    Olivia.   O do not swear!
Hold little faith, though thou hast too much fear.

Enter Sir ANDREW.

    Sir Andrew. For the love of God, a surgeon! Send
one presently to Sir Toby.
    Olivia. What's the matter?
    Sir Andrew. He has broke my head across and has
given Sir Toby a bloody coxcomb too: for the love of God, 180
your help! I had rather than forty pound I were at home.
    Olivia. Who has done this, Sir Andrew?
    Sir Andrew. The count's gentleman, one Cesario: we
took him for a coward, but he's the very devil incardinate.
    Duke. My gentleman Cesario?
    Sir Andrew. 'Od's lifelings, here he is!—You broke
my head for nothing; and that that I did, I was set on
to do't by Sir Toby.
    Viola. Why do you speak to me? I never hurt you: 190
You drew your sword upon me without cause;
But I bespake you fair, and hurt you not.
    Sir Andrew. If a bloody coxcomb be a hurt, you have
hurt me: I think you set nothing by a bloody coxcomb.
Here comes Sir Toby halting,—you shall hear more: but
if he had not been in drink, he would have tickled you
othergates than he did.

Enter Sir TOBY *and* Clown.

    Duke. How now, gentleman! how is't with you?   200
    Sir Toby. That's all one: he has hurt me, and there's
the end on't. Sot, didst see Dick surgeon, sot?

Clown. O, he's drunk, Sir Toby, an hour agone; his eyes were set at eight i' the morning.

Sir Toby. Then he's a rogue and a passy measures pavin: I hate a drunken rogue.

Olivia. Away with him! Who hath made this havoc with them?

210   *Sir Andrew.* I'll help you, Sir Toby, because we'll be dressed together.

Sir Toby. Will you help? an ass-head and a coxcomb and a knave,—a thin-faced knave, a gull!

Olivia. Get him to bed, and let his hurt be look'd to.

           [*Exeunt Clown, Fabian, Sir Toby, and Sir Andrew.*

Enter SEBASTIAN.

  Seb. I am sorry, madam, I have hurt your kinsman;
But, had it been the brother of my blood,
I must have done no less with wit and safety.
You throw a strange regard upon me, and by that
220 I do perceive it hath offended you:
Pardon me, sweet one, even for the vows
We made each other but so late ago.

  Duke. One face, one voice, one habit, and two persons,—
A natural perspective, that is and is not!

  Sebastian. Antonio, O my dear Antonio!
How have the hours rack'd and tortur'd me,
Since I have lost thee!

  Antonio. Sebastian are you?

  Sebastian.   Fear'st thou that, Antonio?

  Antonio. How have you made division of yourself?
230 An apple, cleft in two, is not more twin
Than these two creatures. Which is Sebastian?

  Olivia. Most wonderful!

  Sebastian. Do I stand there? I never had a brother;
Nor can there be that deity in my nature,
Of here and every where. I had a sister,
Whom the blind waves and surges have devour'd.—

[*To Viola*] Of charity, what kin are you to me?
What countryman? what name? what parentage?
   Viola. Of Messaline: Sebastian was my father;
Such a Sebastian was my brother too,
So went he suited to his watery tomb.   240
If spirits can assume both form and suit,
You come to fright us.
   Sebastian.   A spirit I am indeed;
But am in that dimension grossly clad
Which from the womb I did participate.
Were you a woman, as the rest goes even,
I should my tears let fall upon your cheek,
And say, "Thrice-welcome, drowned Viola!"
   Viola. My father had a mole upon his brow.
   Sebastian. And so had mine.   250
   Viola. And died that day when Viola from her birth
Had number'd thirteen years.
   Sebastian. O, that record is lively in my soul!
He finished, indeed, his mortal act
That day that made my sister thirteen years.
   Viola. If nothing lets to make us happy both
But this my masculine usurp'd attire,
Do not embrace me till each circumstance .
Of place, time, fortune, do cohere and jump
That I am Viola: which to confirm,   260
I'll bring you to a captain in this town,
Where lie my maiden weeds; by whose gentle help
I was preserv'd to serve this noble count.
All the occurrence of my fortune since
Hath been between this lady and this lord.
   Sebastian. [*To Olivia*] So comes it, lady, you have been
          mistook:
But nature to her bias drew in that.
You would have been contracted to a maid;
Now are you therein, by my life, deceiv'd,—
You are betroth'd both to a maid and man.   270
   Duke. Be not amaz'd; right noble is his blood.

If this be so, as yet the glass seems true,
I shall have share in this most happy wreck.—
[*To Viola*] Boy, thou hast said to me a thousand times
Thou never shouldst love woman like to me.

Viola. And all those sayings will I over-swear;
And all those swearings keep as true in soul
As doth that orbed continent the fire
That severs day from night.

Duke.   Give me thy hand;
280 And let me see thee in thy woman's weeds.

Viola. The captain that did bring me first on shore
Hath my maid's garments: he upon some action
Is now in durance, at Malvolio's suit,
A gentleman and follower of my lady's.

Olivia. He shall enlarge him:—fetch Malvolio hither;
And yet, alas, now I remember me,
They say, poor gentleman, he's much distract.

Re-enter Clown *with a letter, and* FABIAN.

A most extracting frenzy of mine own
From my remembrance clearly banish'd his.—
290 How does he, sirrah?

Clown. Truly, madam, he holds Beelzebub at the stave's
end as well as a man in his case may do: he has here
writ a letter to you; I should have given't you to-day
morning, but as a madman's epistles are no gospels, so
it skills not much when they are delivered.

Olivia. Open't and read it.

Clown. Look, then, to be well edified when the fool
delivers the madman. [*Reads*] "By the Lord, madam,"—
301 *Olivia.* How now! art thou mad?

Clown. No, madam, I do but read madness: an your
ladyship will have it as it ought to be, you must allow *vox*.

Olivia. Prithee, read i' thy right wits.

Clown. So I do, madonna; but to read his right wits
is to read thus: therefore perpend, my princess, and
give ear.

Olivia. [*To Fabian*] Read it you, sirrah.

Fabian. [*Reads*] "By the Lord, madam, you wrong me, 310
and the world shall know it: though you have put me into
darkness and given your drunken cousin rule over me, yet
have I the benefit of my senses as well as your ladyship.
I have your own letter that induced me to the semblance I
put on; with the which I doubt not but to do myself much
right, or you much shame. Think of me as you please. I
leave my duty a little unthought of, and speak out of my
injury.   THE MADLY-USED MALVOLIO."

Olivia. Did he write this?   320

Clown. Ay, madam.

Duke. This savours not much of distraction.

Olivia. See him deliver'd, Fabian; bring him hither.

                                         [*Exit Fabian.*

My lord, so please you, these things further thought on,
To think me as well a sister as a wife,
One day shall crown the alliance on't, so please you,
Here at my house and at my proper cost.

Duke. Madam, I am most apt to embrace your
              offer.—

[*To Viola*] Your master quits you; and for your service
              done him,

So much against the mettle of your sex,   330
So far beneath your soft and tender breeding,
And since you call'd me master for so long,
Here is my hand: you shall from this time be
Your master's mistress.

Olivia.   A sister! you are she.

Re-enter FABIAN, *with* MALVOLIO.

Duke. Is this the madman?

Olivia.   Ay, my lord, this same.—

How now, Malvolio!

Malvolio.   Madam, you have done me wrong,
Notorious wrong.

Olivia.   Have I, Malvolio? no.

Malvolio. Lady, you have. Pray you, peruse that
  letter.
You must not now deny it is your hand:
340 Write from it, if you can, in hand or phrase;
Or say 'tis not your seal, not your invention:
You can say none of this: well, grant it, then,
And tell me, in the modesty of honour,
Why you have given me such clear lights of favour,
Bade me come smiling and cross-garter'd to you,
To put on yellow stockings and to frown
Upon Sir Toby and the lighter people;
And, acting this in an obedient hope,
Why have you suffer'd me to be imprison'd,
350 Kept in a dark house, visited by the priest,
And made the most notorious geck and gull
That e'er invention play'd on? tell me why.
  Olivia. Alas, Malvolio, this is not my writing,
Though, I confess, much like the character:
But out of question 'tis Maria's hand.
And now I do bethink me, it was she
First told me thou wast mad: then cam'st in smiling,
And in such forms which here were presuppos'd
Upon thee in the letter. Prithee, be content:
360 This practice hath most shrewdly pass'd upon thee;
But when we know the grounds and authors of it,
Thou shalt be both the plaintiff and the judge
Of thine own cause.
  Fabian.   Good madam, hear me speak,
And let no quarrel nor no brawl to come
Taint the condition of this present hour,
Which I have wonder'd at. In hope it shall not,
Most freely I confess, myself and Toby
Set this device against Malvolio here,
Upon some stubborn and uncourteous parts
370 We had conceiv'd against him: Maria writ
The letter at Sir Toby's great importance;
In recompense whereof he hath married her.

How with a sportful malice it was follow'd,
May rather pluck on laughter than revenge;
If that the injuries be justly weigh'd
That have on both sides pass'd.

Olivia. Alas, poor fool, how have they baffled thee!

Clown. Why, "some are born great, some achieve
greatness, and some have greatness thrown upon
them." I was one, sir, in this interlude; one Sir Topas, 380
sir; but that's all one. "By the Lord, fool, I am not
mad." But do you remember? "Madam, why laugh
you at such a barren rascal? an you smile not, he's
gagged:" and thus the whirligig of time brings in his
revenges.

Mal. I'll be reveng'd on the whole pack of you.   [*Exit.*

Olivia. He hath been most notoriously abus'd.

Duke. Pursue him, and entreat him to a peace:
He hath not told us of the captain yet: 390
When that is known, and golden time convents,
A solemn combination shall be made
Of our dear souls. Meantime, sweet sister,
We will not part from hence. Cesario, come;
For so you shall be, while you are a man;
But when in other habits you are seen,
Orsino's mistress and his fancy's queen.

                              [*Exeunt all, except Clown.*

Song.

Clo. When that I was and a little tiny boy,
            With hey, ho, the wind and the rain,
        A foolish thing was but a toy,   400
            For the rain it raineth every day.

        But when I came to man's estate,
            With hey, ho, the wind and the rain,
        'Gainst knaves and thieves men shut their gate,
            For the rain it raineth every day.

But when I came, alas, to wive,
  With hey, ho, the wind and the rain,
By swaggering could I never thrive,
  For the rain it raineth every day.

410   But when I came unto my beds,
  With hey, ho, the wind and the rain,
With toss-pots still had drunken heads,
  For the rain it raineth every day.

A great while ago the world begun,
  With hey, ho, the wind and the rain:
But that's all one, our play is done,
  And we'll strive to please you every day.

                              [*Exit.*

NOTES

ABBREVIATIONS:

E. = the English language; G. = *Glossary*.

Several other abbreviations used sometimes in the *Notes* are explained at the beginning of the *Glossary*, in which they occur more frequently. They should be observed; see p. 137.

ACT I.

SCENE I.

At the outset a dramatist should let us know what is supposed to have gone before, and give us some idea of what the play is to be about and who the chief characters are. From the first Scene we learn (1) a good deal about Orsino—we see how dreamy, changeable, "high fantastical" he is; (2) something about Olivia and the relations existing between her and Orsino.

1. Cf. the opening of Scene 4 in Act II. Orsino's love of music not only gives us an aspect of his character; it helps to explain the rapid way in which Viola wins his favour. Cf. her words, I. 2. 59.

music...the food of love; cf. *Antony and Cleopatra*, II. 5. 1, 2:
"Give me some music; music, moody food
Of us that trade in love."

3. *The appetite*, i.e. love.

4. *dying fall*, a cadence that slowly passed away. *fall*, see G.

5. *the sweet sound*, i.e. the gentle murmur of the breeze, "the low sweet hum of the summer air" (Grant White). By a poetical figure of speech this sound, instead of the breeze that causes it, is said to bring ("give") and carry away ("steal") fragrance.

Though the 1st and later Folios all read *sound*, Pope believed that Shakespeare wrote *south* = 'south wind,' a reading adopted by some editors. But (1) *sound* for *south* is not in itself a probable printer's error, nothing in the neighbouring words makes it probable, and it is most improbable that the printer would blunder so at the very outset of his work. The editors of the later Folios clearly did not consider *sound* a blunder in the 1st Folio. (2) The south wind in Shakespeare as in Milton (*Paradise Lost*, XI. 738) typifies storm and rain, and is therefore inappropriate here. Cf. *As You Like It*, III. 5. 50, "foggy south, puffing with wind and rain"; and 1 *Henry IV*, v. 1. 3–6.

9–15. Love (Orsino says) is very susceptible to impressions and very changeable. Love 'receiveth,' i.e. is affected by, some influence, and lo! in a minute the influence loses its power.

9. *quick and fresh*, sensitive and full of life.

10. *that*, seeing that. *capacity*, power of containing.

12. *validity*, value. *pitch*, height, i.e. excellence.

13. *falls into abatement*, loses its value.

14. *shapes*, conceptions. *fancy*, love; see II. 4. 34.

15. *alone*, above everything else. *fantastical*, imaginative.

17, 18. There is a quibble on *hart* (stag) and *heart*, as in *Julius Cæsar*, III. 1. 204, 208; see IV. 1. 63, note. Shakespeare makes his characters jest thus in moments of great emotion as a relief to the feelings. The dying Gaunt puns on his own name, *Richard II*, II. 1. 73–83, just as in the *Ajax* of Sophocles the unhappy Ajax puns on Αἴας and αἰάζειν, 'to cry alas!'

19–23. An allusion to the classical story of the hunter Actæon, who, for gazing indiscreetly on Diana, goddess of the chase, was changed into a stag, and torn to pieces by his hounds on Mt Cithæron. A similar allegorical use of the legend had been made already by Elizabethan writers. Cf. Daniel's *Sonnets to Delia* (1594), v, "My thoughts, like hounds, pursue me to my death." Note how the comparison of Olivia with the goddess is implied.

20. *purg'd the air*; so that he breathed a purer atmosphere in her presence. It is one of those fanciful thoughts, expressed in fanciful language, which characterise Orsino throughout.

22. *fell*, fierce, savage.

24. *might not*, could not, was not allowed.

25. *her handmaid*, i.e. Maria, of whom we shall hear much.

26. *element*, sky; see G. *till seven years' heat*, i.e. for seven summers. Some change to *years hence*.

28. *cloistress*, nun; see G.

30. *brine*, tears; cf. "*salt* water," II. 1. 32. *season*, keep fresh. The metaphor of 'preserving' runs through the three lines.

32. *remembrance*; scan as four syllables, *rememb-e-rance*.

33. *of that fine frame*, a heart so delicately constituted.

34. *to pay*, as to pay.

35. According to classical legend, Cupid, the god of love, had two sorts of arrows ('shafts'), one tipped with *gold* to inspire love, the other with lead to repel love. Cf. *Glosse* to Spenser's *Shepheards Calender*, *March*, "He [Cupid] is sayd to have *shafts*, some leaden, some *golden*."

36. Orsino means that Olivia's love of her husband will swallow up all her affections for other people.

37–39. In the 1st Folio reading there is no comma from *are*

all down to *king*. It seems to me best to insert commas after
supplied and *perfections*, and explain—'when liver, brain...are
all supplied, and her sweet perfections are filled, with the self-
same king.' Some editors print:

> "When liver, brain and heart,
>   These sovereign thrones, are all supplied and fill'd
> (Her sweet perfections) with one self king";

they take the words in brackets as a parenthetic exclamation in
apposition either to *liver, brain and heart* or to *thrones*. Others
bracket the same three words, read *perfection*, and take it in
apposition to the rest of the sentence—'a thing which will prove
her sweet perfection'; they regard the words as an allusion to
the idea that marriage makes perfect or complete the female
nature (cf. II. 4. 42).

37. *liver*; then supposed to be the seat of the passions,
especially of love—see II. 4. 101, II. 5. 106, and cf. *jecur ulcero-
sum* in Horace, *Odes* I. 25. 15; and of courage (cf. III. 2. 22, 66).

39. *perfections*, excellent qualities; cf. I. 5. 315. Scan *perfections* as four syllables. In Shakespeare and in Milton's early
poems the termination -*ion*, especially with words ending in
ction, such as 'perfe*ction*,' 'affe*ction*,' 'distra*ction*,' is often treated
as two syllables; but commonly this occurs at the end of a line.
In Middle English poetry the termination -*ion* was always
treated as two syllables. See I. 5. 315, V. 71. *self* = *self-same*, as
the 2nd Folio reads. Properly *self* meant 'same' (cf. Germ.
selbe), and in Shakespeare is often used so.

Orsino's prophecy about Olivia is soon fulfilled. He himself
is really "in love with being in love," and relishes his love-pains.

SCENE II.

3, 4. *Illyria...Elysium*; probably a pun is intended.

6. i.e. it was only by chance that you yourself were saved.

9. *split*, broke up on the rocks, was wrecked.

10. *those poor number*; Shakespeare treats *number* as a plural
= 'few.' As the Captain speaks he points to the sailors, who have
perhaps moved a little way off while he is speaking to Viola.

11. *driving*, drifting with the wind and waves; cf. '*driving*
rain.'

14. *lived*, kept float; we speak of a ship '*living* through' a
storm, i.e. not sinking.

15. *Arion*; the Folios misprint *Orion*. It is an allusion to the
classical story (a great favourite with Elizabethan writers—see
Midsummer-Night's Dream, II. 1. 150) of the Greek musician
Arion. On one occasion the sailors of a ship in which he was

returning with many treasures from Sicily to his home at Corinth plotted his murder; whereupon he threw himself into the sea, and was carried safely to land by a dolphin which had been touched by the strains of his lute. The notion of dolphins being fond of music is often alluded to in poetry. *Lycidas*.

19–21. i.e. the fact that I escaped gives me a hope (which your words support) that my brother too has escaped.

21. *country*; scan as three syllables, *count-e-ry*; cf. I. I. 32.

25. i.e. noble in nature as in name.

28. Cf. V. 271, where Orsino shows that he knew Viola's father.

30. *late*, lately.

32. *fresh in murmur*, a recent rumour.

33. *the less*, i.e. in rank, not number; cf. *Macbeth*, V. 4. 12, "Both *more* and *less* have given him the revolt," i.e. great people and small.

39. *for whose dear love*, for her great love of whom; *dear* ='heartfelt,' intensifying the idea of *love* (cf. I. 4. 25).

42–44. i.e. and that my true rank ("estate") might not be discovered till it suited me. Viola's plan, it seems, was to take service in some household till she could arrange for her return home. Then she could safely say who she was.

43. *mellow*, ripe; most probably an adjective.

44. *What my estate is*, i.e. *as to* what; dependent on *delivered* ='discovered, made known.'

compass, achieve, bring about.

47. *behaviour* =outward appearance, rather than manners alone.

48, 49. i.e. a fair outside does not always mean a fair inside. We shall find this sentiment turned against Viola herself with very amusing effect later on (III. 4. 399–404).

though that; *that* is often in Shakespeare added to conjunctions without affecting the sense; cf. 'if *that*' (I. 5. 54, 324), 'lest *that*' (III. 4. 384). There seems to be an ellipse in these cases, e.g. 'though *it is the case* that,' 'if *it be the case* that.'

53. *Conceal me what I am*. The dependent clause ("what I am") is a redundant object explanatory of the first object ("me"). Cf. I. 5. 269. So in *Luke* iv. 34, "I know thee who thou art."

54. *such disguise*, i.e. the page's dress. We see afterwards (V. 261–263) how the Captain assisted her.

57–59. Orsino's fondness for music (of which possibly Viola had heard her father speak—cf. 28) has been observed already (I. 1).

59. *allow me*, approve me; see G.

62. *mute*, silent helper. "Eunuch" shows that *mute* implies "Turkish *mute*" (*Hen. V*, I. 2. 232), i.e. a dumb or tongueless officer employed in Turkey for secret purposes, e.g. as executioner.

SCENE III.

5. *cousin* = 'niece'; see G.

7. *let her except before excepted*, let her object ("take *exceptions*") to what has been before objected to. It is a quasi-legal phrase—from Law Lat. *exceptis excipiendis*—which Sir Toby uses in quibbling allusion to Maria's last remark.

10. *confine myself*, i.e. in clothes = 'dress myself'; a word-play.

13. *straps*, leather-slips attached to boots to pull them on with.

20. *tall*, stout, valiant; see G.

21. *to the purpose*; as we say, 'to the point.'

22. *ducat*, a coin then (1602) worth in England 6s. 8d.; see G.

23. *but a year*; i.e. he will spend all his ducats in one year.

25. *a very fool*, a perfect fool; cf. II. 4. 77, "a very opal."

27. *viol-de-gamboys*, the bass-viol; see G.

speaks three or four languages. Sir Toby is rather daring in his praise of his friend, for Sir Andrew has to enquire the meaning of *pourquoi*, and confesses that he neglected "the tongues" (95–97).

30. A *natural* meant a fool (cf. *The Tempest*, III. 2. 37), and Maria quibbles on the two possible senses, (1) 'naturally, by nature,' (2) 'like a fool.' Some change needlessly to *all most natural*.

32, 33. *allay the gust*, appease his taste for (Lat. *gustus*). We shall have later on an illustration of Sir Andrew's quarrelsomeness.

37. *substractors*; he means *detractors*. Cf. the mistakes that Bottom makes in *Midsummer-Night's Dream* through his love of long words, e.g. 'exposition' for 'disposition,' IV. 1. 43. Sheridan's famous character Mrs *Malaprop* (F. *mal-à-propos*) in the comedy of *The Rivals* has given her name to verbal blunders—*malapropisms*, as we say—of this kind. Her errors (e.g. 'epitaph' for 'epithet') are diverting.

43. *coystril*, a mean paltry fellow; see G.

44. "A large *top* was formerly kept in every village, to be whipped in frosty weather, that the peasants might be kept warm by exercise, and out of mischief, while they could not work."

Castiliano vulgo. Warburton proposed *volto*—'put on your Castilian countenance, i.e. grave solemn looks.' Even if that was what Sir Toby wished to say, Shakespeare probably intended that he should blunder (as in line 37). Most likely, however, Sir Toby in his desire to impress Maria merely coined a phrase which had a fine foreign sound. *Castiliano* (Spanish *Castellano*, 'belonging to Castile') and *Castile* are used by Elizabethans in exclamatory phrases; it seems to have been a piece of Elizabethan slang, perhaps "adopted immediately after the defeat of the Armada, and...expressive of jollity." Perhaps Sir Toby means: '*Now* (with the bibulous Sir Andrew coming) we shall be a rollicking Castilian crowd: no use your chiding me for drinking: look out, rather, for the Castilian touch.'

53. *What's that?*, what does *accost* (see G.) mean? The stupid Sir Andrew is constantly mistaking or asking the meaning of things; cf. 80, 95.

65. *an*, if; see G. *let part*, let *her* depart; cf. v. 394.

67, 68. *An you part so...* Note how Sir Andrew echoes the words of Sir Toby and follows his lead; cf. II. 3. 176, 177 (about Maria's "device"), II. 5. 200–210.

69. *fools in hand*, fools to deal with. Maria quibbles in reply.

71. *Marry*, see G.

73. *Now, sir.* Of course, she takes Sir Andrew's hand and hints (but he does not see her meaning) that *now* she does think that she has a "fool in hand" (69).

thought is free; a proverbial saying very apt here since it echoes Sir Andrew's "do you *think*" in 68. Cf. *The Tempest*, III. 2. 132.

74. "*The bringing the hand to the buttery-bar, and letting it drink*, is a proverbial phrase among forward Abigails [maid-servants], to ask at once for a kiss and a present."— Kenrick. *buttery-bar*, see G.

77. *It's dry*, i.e. the hand; this was considered a sign that the owner of the hand was indifferent to love.

80. *what's your jest?* He does not understand what she meant by *dry* in 77. In the next line 81 *dry* = 'stupid,' as in I. 5. 45. Cf. *Love's Labour's Lost*, v. 2. 373, "This *jest* is *dry* to me."

83. *at my fingers' ends.* Another word-play or quibble. She means (1) that she is always ready with a joke, (2) that she has hold of Sir Andrew, who is certainly very "dry" (=stupid). A point like this is much clearer when the play is acted. Here, for instance, an actress could raise Sir Andrew's hand high up and then suddenly drop it. Such a gesture would make "at my fingers' ends" quite clear.

84. *barren*, i.e. of jests; she has no more to make.

85. *lackest*, needest, i.e. to cheer him. *canary*, i.e. wine; see G.

86. *put down*; humiliated, made to look foolish.

90. *eater of beef*; Shakespeare was thinking of his own coun-trymen. It was a stock joke against the English that they liked "great meals of beef," as the Constable of France says in

Henry V, III. 7. 161. "Beef-witted" is a term of reproach in *Troilus and Cressida*, II. 1. 14. Curious notions prevailed then as to the effect of food upon the character; a great authority on them is Burton's *Anatomy of Melancholy* (1621). He says that beef produces melancholy (I. 95, ed. 1800).

94. *ride home*; we hear of his horse "gray Capilet," III. 4. 315.

97. *the tongues*, languages; cf. *Much Ado About Nothing*, V. 1. 167, "he hath the tongues," i.e. is a good linguist. Perhaps Sir Andrew pronounces *tongues* oddly: anyhow Sir Toby puns upon *tongues* and *tongs* (i.e. curling-tongs), a joke lost upon his friend. In *Coriolanus*, III. 1. 35, the 2nd Folio has *tongs* for *tongues*.

98. *bear-baiting*; see II. 5. 9, note. The Bear Garden on the Bankside in Southwark, close to the Globe Theatre, was a very popular London resort, till 1642, when it was closed.

118. *there's life in't*, it is not a hopeless case; cf. *Lear*, IV. 6. 206.

121. *masques*; see G. *revels*, festivities; see G.

122. *kickshawses*, trifles; see G.

126. *old*; 'practised'; we speak of a man being 'an *old* hand' at something. Sir Andrew will not compare himself with an expert or with his "betters." He is self-diffident, which makes him look up to the self-confident Sir Toby. Theobald suggested *a nobleman* (i.e. Orsino).

127, 130. *galliard*, a quick dance; see G. Quibbling allusions to eating *capers* (a sort of pickle) with boiled mutton and to the dancing movement called the *capriole* (goat's leap).

131. *the back-trick*, a caper backwards in dancing.

133. *Wherefore are these things hid?* He argues, 'Why not display these gifts and accomplishments, so that Olivia may see them? Why go home and let them be hidden? Stay a little longer and enjoy these "kickshawses".' One reason, perhaps the chief, why Sir Toby wants Sir Andrew to remain is that he may get more money out of him.

134, 135. *a curtain...picture*. In picture galleries and continental churches the finest pictures are often protected by curtains from light, dust, etc. See again I. 5. 251 (where Olivia unveils herself).

135. Possibly *Mistress Mall* is as imaginary as the Clown's philosopher Quinapalus (I. 5. 39). Some personal allusion, however, seems intended, and Steevens suggested that it was to a well-known Elizabethan character, Mary Frith, commonly called "*Mall* (or Moll) Cutpurse" from her celebrity as a thief. She is constantly mentioned in contemporary works (rather later, however, than *Twelfth Night*), and is introduced as a character

in more than one play. The accounts vary as to the date of her birth, Malone placing it in 1584 and other writers in 1589: the latter date makes it quite, and the former almost, impossible that she should have become celebrated by 1601, the probable date of *Twelfth Night*. But a casual allusion like this may well have been inserted some time after the *first* production of the play; and on this principle I am inclined to think that she is referred to here. *Mall* is a diminutive of *Mary*.

137. *galliard...coranto*; see each word in G.

142. *under the star*. It was then a popular belief that the characters, bodies and fortunes of men were influenced by the star under which they were born. In *Lear*, I. 2. 128–144 Shakespeare makes Edmund ridicule these astrological notions, and doubtless he himself did not believe in them, though they are often referred to in his plays. Cf. I. 4. 35, II. 1. 3–5, II. 5. 156 ("in my stars"), 184 ("my stars be praised"); and see *malignant* in G.

the star of a galliard. Sir Toby humorously suggests that the influence of some special star enables men to excel in the galliard.

143. *does indifferent well*, looks pretty well.

144. *flame-coloured stock*, bright yellow stocking (i.e. such as Malvolio puts on, III. 4). The Folios have *dam'd-colour'd*. Most editors read *flame-coloured*, found in 1 *Henry IV*, I. 2. 11, and often in the 17th century dramatists; some prefer *damask-coloured*, i.e. red.

147. *born under Taurus*. See 142, note. According to one branch of astrology (medical astrology) each of the 12 signs of the Zodiac controlled a particular portion of the human body and its affections. This notion is seen in the diagrams of some old-fashioned almanacs. Really *Taurus* was thought to govern the neck and throat.

SCENE IV.

The humour and interest of the Scenes in which Viola is with Olivia and Orsino turn largely upon the fact that they do not know her to be a girl while the audience does. Shakespeare purposely makes Olivia and Orsino say things (cf. lines 30–34) which have for the audience a point whereof the speaker is quite unconscious. It is a dramatic artifice similar to the "irony" which Greek dramatists employ. In the same way many of Viola's remarks (cf. III. 1. 169–172) contain veiled allusions to her sex which the audience perceives at once, whereas Olivia or Orsino sees no allusion at all.

2. *much advanced*, promoted to a high position. We have seen one reason why Cesario (Viola) was likely to win Orsino's favour.

3. *three days*. A time-reference, showing how long has elapsed since Scene 2; and probably Scenes 1–3 took place on the same day.

5. *fear his humour*, i.e. that he is changeable, capricious; cf. *As You Like It*, I. 2. 278, "the duke is humorous"=capricious.

11. *On your attendance*, I await your orders.

12. *Stand you*; the courtiers. He addresses Cesario (Viola) as *thou* (13), a sign of familiarity; cf. *tu* in French, *du* in German.

13. *but*=than; used so after *negative* comparatives; cf. II. 5. 201.

13, 14. Cf. I *Henry IV*, I. 3. 188, "And now I will unclasp a secret book" (said by Worcester when he reveals his scheme to Hotspur).

16. Scan *accéss*, as usually in Shakespeare. See G.

21. *civil bounds*, bounds of civility or good manners. Cf. *Julius Cæsar*, I. 2. 9, "sterile curse"=curse of sterility; IV. 2. 16, "familiar instances"=instances (signs) of familiarity. In such phrases (frequent in Shakespeare) the adjective defines the noun's sphere or character: thus the curse consists in sterility, the instance (sign) is one of familiarity. In German this relation would be expressed by a compound noun.

23. *say I*, suppose that I.

25. *dear faith*, heartfelt devotion. *dear*; cf. I. 2. 39, note.

27. *attend*, pay attention to. His prediction is fulfilled too truly.

28. *nuncio*, messenger; see G. Scan *aspéct* always in Shakespeare.

31. *thou art a man*, arrived at manhood; note the "irony" here.

32. *rubious*, ruddy. *pipe*, voice; properly throat, wind-pipe. *small*; used of a clear, treble voice; cf. *Midsummer-Night's Dream*, I. 2. 52, "you may speak small," i.e. like a woman.

33. *sound*, clear in tone; some change to "shrill *in* sound."

34. i.e. everything about you resembles a woman. *part*, character. The fact that on the Elizabethan stage female parts were acted by young men or boys made these disguises a favourite dramatic device.

35. *constellation*, character (as influenced by the stars).

39, 40. *as freely*; connect with *to call*. Cesario (Viola) shall be as much master of Orsino's fortunes as Orsino himself.

41, 42. The fact that Viola is in love with Orsino has to be made plain at the outset because it lends so much more point to the Scenes between them, and also to the Scenes between Olivia and Viola. *Twelfth Night* is a play of "loves at first sight."

41. *barful*, full of bars, i.e. impediments.

Scene V.

3. *in way of thy excuse*, to make excuses for thee (to Olivia).

6. *to fear no colours*, to fear no foe, to have no fears; a common Elizabethan phrase, in which *colours* = flags, i.e. of an enemy; cf. *in the wars* (12), which keeps up the military metaphor. He quibbles on *colours* and *collars*, i.e. halters, in which to be "well hanged." So in 2 *Henry IV*, v. 5. 92.

7. *make that good*, prove what you say.

9. *lenten*, meagre, poor (like meagre Lenten food).

21. *for turning away*, as for being dismissed. To lose his place in Olivia's house would be less disagreeable in summer than in winter. This indicates the time of year in which the events of the play happen.

bear it out, make it (his dismissal) supportable.

27. *gaskins*, loose breeches; fastened to the doublet by laces called *points*: hence Maria's pun. *gaskin*; a corruption of Ital. *Grechesco*, 'Greekish,' used of a kind of hose brought from Greece into Venice.

29. *Sir Toby*; a hint that he might marry Maria.

34. *You were best*, you had best. Cf. II. 2. 27, "she were better," and III. 4. 12, "your ladyship were best." This idiom represents an impersonal construction changed into a personal. Thus "*I* were best" (*Cymbeline*, III. 6. 19) would in earlier English have been "*me* were best" = 'to me it were best.' People misunderstood that (1) *me* was a dative, (2) the sentence was impersonal, and substituted *I* which seemed more correct. The impersonal constructions so largely used in Old English were becoming less familiar to the Elizabethans.

35. *Wit*; he apostrophises wit as though it were a goddess.

39. *Quinapalus*. It is part of the Clown's professional humour to invent characters with sonorous names, such as this philosopher Quinapalus and "Pigrogromitus" (II. 3. 23). Sometimes he fathers on them the proverbs and nonsensical maxims of which he is so fond; cf. IV. 2. 15. Dickens makes Sam Weller in *Pickwick* employ a similar device.

45. *dry*, stupid; cf. I. 3. 81.

46. *dishonest*, because he absents himself so much from the house.

47. *madonna*, my lady; see G.

51. *botcher*, patcher, mender; used oftener of a tailor than of a cobbler. Cf. *Coriolanus*, II. 1. 98.

55. *syllogism*, form of reasoning.

61. *misprision*, mistake; see G.

62. *cucullus non facit monachum*, "a cowl does not make a

monk" (a common proverb); so, though the Clown wore a
Fool's dress (=*motley*; see G.), yet that did not make him a fool
as regards his brain. The Elizabethan Fool had a suit of red and
yellow alternately; a hood (caricaturing the monk's cowl) with
an ass's ears and a cock's crest; and a "bauble" or mock-sceptre
ending in a fool's head.

66. *dexteriously*; the Clown's mistake for *dexterously*
('adroitly').

69. *good my mouse*; the pronoun is often transposed thus in
short phrases of address. *mouse*, a term of endearment; cf.
Hamlet, III. 4. 183, "call you his *mouse*."

70. *idleness*, frivolous occupation.

84. *God send you, sir*. The Clown's wishes are fulfilled sooner
than he anticipates.

86. *pass his word*, pledge his word. Cf. *Titus Andronicus*,
I. 468, "I have *passed* my *word* and *promise* to the emperor."

89–96. *I marvel...zanies*. The Clown does not forget this
speech, and Malvolio will have occasion to recall it (v. 382–384).

90. *barren*, i.e. of brains ='dull.'

put down with, i.e. by; *with*=*by* is common in Shakespeare.

93. *out of his guard*, off his guard: metaphor of fencing.

94. *minister occasion*, supply him with a topic of jesting.

94, 95. *I protest, I take*. Really a reproof to Olivia for praising
the Clown (80), and indeed for keeping him at all. Olivia in her
reply snubs Malvolio for his implied impertinence.

I take...no better, I value, regard them as no better.

95. *these kind*; cf. *those...number* in I. 2. 10, and *Lear*, II. 2. 107,
"these kind of knaves." The pronoun is 'attracted' to the plural
idea of the whole phrase. *set*, professional, kept for the purpose
of jesting.

96. *zanies*, stupid imitators; see G.

97. *sick of self-love*. A noticeable phrase; it describes the
failing in Malvolio's character so precisely.

100. The *bird-bolt* was a short arrow; see G.

Olivia means that Malvolio takes things too seriously—a
common failing with people who have no sense of humour.

101–104. *There is no slander....* 'Just as a professional fool is
privileged ("allowed") to say what he likes, so is a discreet man
privileged to reprove as much as he likes: the one will not be
accused of slander, nor the other of railing.' A sarcastic hit at
Malvolio who is certainly "discreet" and inclined to "reprove."

The Elizabethan Jester was allowed to joke at the expense
of his superiors (like the Fool in *King Lear*) but with tact, as
Viola says (III. I. 67–74). And of course he made puns.

105, 106. *Mercury*, the patron deity of lying. *leasing*, the practice of telling lies, falsehood; see G. The Clown hints that Olivia has spoken well of fools at the expense of truth.

108. *much desires*; understand *who*; cf. 123 and see p. 157.

109. *From the Count?* She has had so many messages from Orsino.

111. *well attended*; cf. Orsino's directions in the last Scene (36, 37).

115. *speaks...madman.* Cf. *Henry V*, v. 2. 156, "I speak to thee plain soldier," i.e. in the style of one. The accusative is cognate, as in 'play the madman.'

122, 123. *here he comes, one of thy kin, has.* So many editors read. The Folios have a full stop after *comes*. *has*, i.e. *who* has.

123. *pia mater*, brain; properly the inner membrane covering the brain, the exterior one (of firmer texture) being called the *dura mater*.

129. *sot*; 'stupid fellow, fool'; cf. F. *sot*, foolish. In modern English *sot* is a more offensive word, implying drunkenness, than in Shakespeare. *these...herring*; cf. *salmon, trout* used as plurals.

137. *it's all one*; cf. v. 201, 416; 'it's all the same.'

140. *heat*, thirst; *above heat*, more than thirst requires.

141. Cf. *Richard II*, v. 5. 61, "This music *mads* me" (maddens).

142, 143. *crowner*, coroner; see G. *sit on*, hold an inquest on.

149. *takes on him to understand*, pretends to know.

157. "At the *doors of sheriffs* usually *posts* were set up, on which proclamations were fixed," and which served to denote an official residence. Often they were ornamental, too, being carved and painted.

166. *squash*, unripe peascod (=the pod that holds the peas).

167. *codling*, any unripe apple; now =a special kind of apple.

168. *in standing water.* Some editors read *e'en* for *in.* The metaphor of the sea between ebb and flood implies an intermediate state; "at the turn of the tide." Cf. *The Tempest*, II. 1. 221.

169. *well-favoured*, good-looking; see G. The description apparently influences Olivia and leads her to admit the messenger.

170. *shrewishly*, sharply, i.e. like a *shrew* (a scolding woman).

171. *were scarce out*; perhaps the verb is 'attracted' to the subjunctive mood of the previous verb "one *would* think."

181–188. The Elizabethan courtier's fanciful, euphuistic style.

186. *con*, learn by heart, as an actor his speeches; cf. Wordsworth, *Ode on Intimations of Immortality*, 102, "The little *actor cons* another *part*." The metaphor of the stage is kept up in "out of my *part*" =actor's *rôle* (191), "comedian" (194), "that I *play*" (197).

187, 188. *comptible*, sensitive. *sinister usage*, discourtesy.

195. *heart*; a friendly form of address; cf. II. 3. 16, 110.

197. *I am not that I play*; an allusion which the audience (but not Olivia) understands.

200. She "usurps" herself in not giving herself to Orsino.

201. *this is from*, away from, not part of, my message.

204. *forgive you the praise*, excuse you from saying it.

207, 208. *poetical...feigned*. Cf. *As You Like It*, III. 3. 20, "the truest poetry is the most feigning"; but there *feign* has the good sense 'imagination,' while here 'pretence' is implied.

211. *If you be not mad*. So the Folios; many editors omit *not*. Retaining *not*, I think that the passage illustrates what Cowden Clarke in his note on it terms Shakespeare's "*apparent* antitheses." Olivia seems to be speaking hurriedly, and she may think that there is some antithesis between *if you be not mad* and *if you have reason*, though really the antithesis is one of sound, not sense. What she says comes to this—'if you have any sense, go, or, at least, be brief.' To omit *not* gives a more logical sense; but people speaking under the influence of excitement are not always logical. Errors of this kind are often much truer to human nature than their corrections.

213. *not that time of moon*, I am not in the humour to.

214. *skipping*, flighty, flippant.

217. *swabber*; a sailor who washes the deck of a vessel with a *swab* or mop; cf. *The Tempest*, II. 2. 48, "The master, the swabber, the boatswain and I." Perhaps the word is applied to Maria because she tried to clear Viola out of the room, by hinting to her to go, just as a *swabber* clears the deck. At any rate, the nautical metaphor (cf. "hull") was due to Maria's "hoist sail." *hull*, float; see G.

218. *some mollification for*; 'pray pacify your *giant* here,' a satirical reference to the height of Maria ("the *little* villain," II. 5. 16), and possibly an allusion to the fact that in old romances and fairy tales the heroines are often protected by giants.

223. *your office*, what you were commissioned to say.

224. *It alone*, i.e. it concerns your ear alone.

225. *taxation*, demand, claim.

226. *olive*; the traditional symbol of peace.

231. *entertainment*, reception (viz. by Sir Toby, Malvolio, Maria).

239. *comfortable*, comforting; see G.

252. *Such a one I was this present*; so the Folios read—if rightly, with the sense (it seems), 'that is how I looked a moment ago,' i.e. before she veiled herself at Viola's entrance. Perhaps the best emendation is, "*as* this presents" = 'represents'; but

Shakespeare elsewhere uses the phrase *this present* = 'the present time, this moment.' Herford says: "this picture shews what I was *all this time*."

254. *if God did all*, if it is all natural, not painted. Shakespeare often refers to the practice of painting the face; cf. *Hamlet*, V. 1. 213.

255. *'Tis in grain*, it is dyed with a fast colour. Some explain, 'it is natural, ingrained.' See G.

258. *cunning*; used by Shakespeare often in the good sense 'skilful.'

259–261. A favourite idea of Elizabethan poets, that those who possess personal beauty should marry and through their children enable that beauty to remain in the world instead of dying out. Shakespeare's *Sonnets* 1–17 treat this theme under different metaphors, that of a "copy" (261) or reprint occurring in *Sonnet* 11.

259. *she*, woman; cf. *As You Like It*, III. 2. 10, "The fair, the chaste and unexpressive she." So *he* = man; cf. *3 Henry VI*, . 1. 46.

262–268. A compliment is embarrassing to a refined and sensitive person. Note with what good taste Olivia turns aside Viola's pretty speeches, feigning a half-sarcastic indifference and self-depreciation.

263. *schedules*, lists, inventories; a legal word (see IV. 1. 36).

265. *labelled to my will*, appended to my will and testament.

266. *gray*; then a favourite colour for women's eyes. Chaucer's Prioresse had "eyen greye as glas" (a phrase that became proverbial). The Elizabethans disliked very dark eyes or hair in women; Shakespeare alludes to this prejudice often; see especially *Sonnet* 127.

268. *praise*, in both senses 'commend' and 'appraise, estimate.'

269. *I see you what you are*; cf. 1. 2. 53, note.

271–273. i.e. his love is so great that the fairest woman could but give him a reward such as he well deserves. The emphatic word is *recompensed*; cf. 304.

273. *the nonpareil of*, the peerless queen, the paragon of; see G.

274. A short line, of four accents, either through the dropping out of some word (e.g. a second *with*), or purposely—such lines being found "where a number of short clauses or epithets are connected together in one line, and must be pronounced slowly" (Abbott).

275. Cf. the picture in *As You Like It*, II. 7. 148, of the lover "*sighing* like furnace." See II. 2. 40, 4. 64–66.

276–282. Orsino resembles Olivia too much to attract her; thus his sentimental love is like her sentimental grief. Attraction lies rather in opposite qualities.

279. *in voices well divulged*, well spoken of by people.

280. *dimension*, body, person; cf. v. 244.

281. *gracious*, attractive.

283. *in my master's flame*, with my master's ardent passion.

287. *Make me*, for me (myself). *willow*; a symbol of unhappy love; cf. the old ballad "Sing willow, willow," *Othello*, iv. 3. 41–56.

289. *cantons*, songs; see G.

291. *reverberate*, resounding; literally 'made to resound.' For the participial termination *-ate* = *-ated* see *distract* in G.

293, 294. i.e. her name should be echoed from earth to air.

295. Note how the vehemence of Viola's outburst impresses Olivia.

300. *you*; said with some emphasis.

303. *feed post*, paid messenger.

305. i.e. 'may love make the heart of that man whom.' Viola's wish, we shall see, is fulfilled.

that; the antecedent is contained in *his* (='of him'); cf. iii. 1. 69.

make; the optative or imperative use of the subjunctive was commoner then than now. Cf. "*be* this" = *may* this be, 330.

307. *cruelty*, cruel person. Abstract used for concrete; cf. *conduct* = conductor, *diligence* = diligent servant, *The Tempest*, v. 244, 241.

310. Sir Toby too sees that Viola is well-born (iii. 4. 203).

312. *do give thee...blazon*, serve as a coat of arms to thee, i.e. as a sign of high birth; see G. Why *fivefold*?

313. *unless*. The sense seems to be 'if only the master were'; or perhaps she is saying to herself "I could never marry Orsino," and then adds aloud "unless the master were the man," i.e. unless they could be exchanged. The sentence is purposely left incomplete, only bits of her thoughts being given us.

315. *perfections*; for its sense and scansion cf. i. 1. 39, note.

315–317. *feel...to creep*; cf. iii. 1. 120, "*hear* you *to* solicit." Verbs of perception, 'feel,' 'see,' 'hear,' are often followed by *to* in Shakespeare.

319. *peevish*, saucy; see G. She misleads Malvolio purposely.

320. *county's*, count's; see G. The Folios have *countes* or *counts*.

324, 325. She half tells him to bid Viola (as he does) come again.

329. *owe*, possess and so 'have control of'; see G.

Young students sometimes misunderstand Viola's position as a "page" and picture Olivia wooing "a page-boy." It may not be amiss therefore to give Dr Murray's definition of "page" in its courtly sense: "A youth employed as the personal attendant of a person of rank. In earlier times often himself of gentle birth [cf. 297, 298] and placed in this position in order to be trained in the usages of good society." Cesario is a "page" in that sense; the equal of Valentine and Curio ("gentlemen attending on the Duke"), though not the equal of the Duke or Countess.

ACT II.

Scene I.

1. *nor...not*; the double negative expresses his *emphatic* entreaty.

3. *my stars shine darkly*, fortune is unkind to me; see 1. 3. 142.

4. *malignancy*, malevolence; see G.

5. *distemper*, put out of temper, make ill-humoured.

11. *sooth*, truly, indeed; see G.

12. *determinate*, resolved upon. *extravagancy*, vagrancy. Cf. *extravagant* used in its literal sense 'wandering,' *Othello*, 1. 1. 137. Lat. *extra*, 'beyond,' + *vagari*, 'to wander.'

13. *touch of modesty*, i.e. strain, trait, of modesty.

15. *it charges me in manners*, I am obliged as a matter of courtesy.

16. *to express myself*, to make myself known.

You must know. This account is intended to let the audience know more about Viola and Sebastian and the shipwreck. One of the difficulties of a dramatist is to give information necessary to the understanding of the plot and yet to do it in an indirect way, so that the spectators shall not feel that they are being instructed. When the audience are conscious that the action of the play is brought to a standstill so that the circumstances of the plot may be explained, then the illusion is destroyed.

18. *Messaline*, an imaginary locality; Capell proposed *Mitylene*.

19. *you have heard of*. Sebastian's father was so well known.

20. *in an hour*, i.e. in *one* hour. It is generally after a preposition that *a* or *an* = 'one'; cf. *Othello*, II. 3. 212, "both at *a* birth."

22. Cf. *Comedy of Errors*, III. 1. 122, "I'll meet you...*some hour* hence," i.e. *about* an hour. This use of *some* with a singular noun of time may arise through its use before numerals as in

"*some sixteen* months," *Two Gentlemen of Verona*, IV. I. 21.
(Abbott, p. 30.)

23. *breach*, surf; or perhaps the place where the waves break.

27. *She much resembled me.* This is said so as to prepare the
audience for the likeness between Viola and Sebastian.

was yet, i.e. *who* was; see I. 5. 108, note.

of many; *of* = 'by' is common in Shakespeare after passive verbs.

28. Most editors take *estimable* = 'esteeming,' and *wonder* =
'admiration,' and interpret, 'with so high a degree of admiration.'
Cf. *deceivable* = 'deceiving,' IV. 3. 21. It seems to me not impossible that *estimable wonder* = 'wonder of estimation,' i.e.
excessive admiration; like *civil bounds* = 'bounds of civility,'
I. 4. 21.

overfar believe, go too far and believe. Sebastian wishes to
undo the compliment which he paid himself when he said that
his sister was considered very like him—and beautiful.

34. He makes this apology, having learnt Sebastian's high
rank.

35. *your trouble*, the trouble caused to you.

36, 37. Antonio loves Sebastian so much that to be refused
permission to accompany him will be like a death-blow.

41. *kindness*, tenderness. *I am yet*, i.e. still; he has not recovered from the loss of his sister.

42. "And all *my mother* came into mine eyes
          And gave me up to tears" (*Henry V*, IV. 6. 31, 32).

46. *I have many enemies*; this is explained later (III. 3. 26–37).

SCENE II.

5. *this ring.* See I. 5. 320, 321.

6. *to have taken*, by having taken: a gerund, not infinitive.

9. *She will none of*; see I. 3. 113, note.

12. *taking of this*, receiving of the ring back. That was not
exactly the point as to which Olivia wanted to see Orsino's
messenger again; cf. I. 5. 324, 325.

13. *the ring.* Some editors read "*no* ring"; but Viola dis-
sembles because she instinctively guesses Olivia's secret (cf.
18–42), and wishes to conceal it from Malvolio. If she said
"*no* ring," his suspicions might be roused. Viola's love of
Orsino, and her woman's quickness, enable her to read the
symptoms of love in others.

15. *so returned*, i.e. in the same way, viz. thrown on the
ground.

16. *in your eye*, in your sight, right before you.

19. *forbid...not*; a negative after a verb expressing negation,

as in French. Cf. *Richard III*, I. 3. 90, "You may *deny* that you
were *not* the cause" (i.e. that you *were*). The idiom springs from
the same love of emphasis that gives us the double negative
(II. 1. 1).

21. *lost*, caused her to lose control of.

27. *she were better*; see I. 5. 34, note.

29. *the pregnant enemy*, the ever-ready foe of man, viz. Satan.
Cf. III. 4. 109, and *Macbeth*, III. 1. 69, "the common *enemy of
man*." The name *Satan* means 'adversary.'

30. *the proper-false*, men who are at once handsome ("proper")
and deceitful; cf. *beauteous-evil*, III. 4. 403. Compound adjec-
tives, in which the first adj. qualifies the second adverbially, are
not uncommon in Shakespeare; cf. 'daring-hardy' in *Richard II*,
I. 3. 43, 'childish-foolish' in *Richard III*, I. 3. 142.

31. *set their forms*, stamp their image; the metaphor of sealing
(cf. *waxen*='soft, impressible').

33. The Folios read "are made, *if* such we bee." *be*, see G.

34. *fadge*, turn out, prosper; see G.

35. *fond*; probably a verb='dote'; but *am* might be understood.

37–40. As a page, she is fatal to Orsino's prospect of winning
Olivia's love: as a woman, she will make Olivia sigh all in vain.

Scene III.

The time of this Scene is the night of the same day as the last
Scene. Cf. 143, "the youth of the count's was *today* with my
lady."

2. *betimes*, early; literally *by time*.

diluculo surgere, i.e. *saluberrimum est*, "to rise early is most
healthful"—a maxim quoted from Lilly's *Latin Grammar*. This
was a school-book in general use during Shakespeare's life, and,
no doubt, he had learnt from it as a boy at Stratford Grammar
School. Every educated man in Shakespeare's audience would
know the maxim, so we can imagine the laugh at Sir Andrew's
reply, "Nay...I know not," and Sir Toby's flattering "Thou'rt
a *scholar*" (13).

7. *can*, vessel to hold wine or ale.

10. *elements*; see G. Sir Toby was going to suggest that they
should replenish the liquid "element" in them.

14. *Marian*. So the Folios; some editors read *Maria* (cf. 129).
The change is not necessary; Malvolio calls her *Mary* in one
place (130), *Maria* in another (II. 5. 27). *Marian* is a form of
Maria or *Mary*. *stoup*, or *stoop*, a drinking cup, flagon; Dutch
stoop, 'a large cup.'

16. *my hearts*, my good friends; cf. 110 and see I. 5. 195, note.

17. "I believe Shakespeare had in his thoughts a common sign [i.e. sign-board of an inn], in which *two* wooden heads are exhibited, with this inscription under it, '*We three* loggerheads be' [i.e. fools]. The spectator or reader is supposed to make the third. The Clown means to insinuate, that Sir Toby and Sir Andrew had as good a title to the name of *fool* as himself." —Malone.

18, 19. *catch*, part-song, glee; see G. *breast*, voice; see G.

20. See v. 180, and cf. *Merry Wives of Windsor*, I. 1. 205, "I had rather than *forty* shillings I had my Book of Songs here." Note that *forty* is used constantly by Elizabethans as a significant number, where no precise reckoning is needed. Cf. *Sonnet* 2, "When forty winters shall besiege thy brow," and *Coriolanus*, III. 1. 243, "I could beat forty of them." I have no doubt that this use arose from the fact that forty is a mysterious number in Scripture, and associated with many great events. Thus the wanderings of the Israelites lasted forty years, the fast of our Lord forty days—likewise the fast of Elijah (1 *Kings* xix. 8), and the stay of Moses on the Mount (*Exodus* xxiv. 18).

23–25. *Pigrogromitus*. Much that the Clown says is intentional nonsense, one point of which is that it ridicules the use of affected, stilted language. As to his trick of bringing in long imaginary names, perhaps to impress Sir Andrew, see I. 5. 39, note. Some critics find in it an imitation of Rabelais.

26. *leman*, sweetheart; the Folios *lemon*; a certain correction.

27–29. *impeticos thy gratillity*; he may have meant *impeticoat thy gratuity*, i.e. put your gift in my pocket. These domestic Fools often wore long coats which might be humorously called 'petticoats.' But the whole speech is mere "fooling"—as even Sir Andrew sees. *whipstock*, the handle of a whip. Perhaps there is a hint that Malvolio is sharp at scenting out things.

Myrmidons; a race of warriors who followed Achilles to the Trojan war; used colloquially ='followers or ministers' e.g. legal officers.

31. *when all is done*, after all.

34. *testril*, sixpence; see G. *of*, from.

35. "If one knight gives, *another should*." Either these words have dropped out in the printing or the Clown interrupted Sir Andrew.

37. *of good life*, i.e. a song of a sober moral kind.

40–53. This Song is found in Morley's *Consort Lessons*, printed in 1599, i.e. before the probable date of *Twelfth Night*. Most likely it was an old ballad not composed by Shakespeare; popular ballads were then often introduced thus into plays.

But possibly Shakespeare was the author and re-used the song when he came to write this play.

We may note here the number of songs referred to in this Scene, especially in 76–110. The constant mention or introduction of ballads old and new is a marked feature of the Elizabethan drama. A great quantity of these ballads has survived in popular song-books and collections of airs. They support other evidence which shows that in Shakespeare's time the English were a very musical race, and that a knowledge of music was widespread. Some think that Puritanism (e.g. by its hostility to Church music) had much to do with the decline of music in England as a national taste and recreation. Percy's *Reliques of Ancient English Poetry* gives versions of several of the songs in *Twelfth Night*. Dramatically the great feature of the songs in Shakespeare's plays is their appropriateness to their context.

43. *sweeting*, sweet one; cf. *Othello*, II. 3. 252, "All's well, sweeting."

51. i.e. delay leads to no good.

52. *sweet and twenty*, probably a term of endearment, literally ='twenty times sweet.' But some explain it 'give me sweet kisses and twenty of them'; others as formed like 'sweet seventeen' (*years* understood).

55. Sir Toby, it seems, talks so absurdly to lead Sir Andrew on to talk equally, or more, absurdly.

59. *make the welkin dance*, "drink till the sky seems to turn round" (Johnson). *welkin*, see G.

61. In *Much Ado*, II. 3. 59–62, when Balthasar plays on the lute, Benedick says, "now is his *soul ravish'd*," and then remarks how strange it is that music "should *hale* [="draw"] *souls out of men's bodies*," i.e. should affect them so strongly. This "catch" is to be so good that even a Puritanical psalm-singing weaver would be transported by it: not one soul, but three, would be "haled from his body" (a touch of exaggeration, to emphasise the charming effect of the music). Sir Toby chooses a weaver because Elizabethan weavers were proverbial for their love of psalms and hymns (the very opposite of catches!); many were Calvinist refugees from the Netherlands. See 1 *Hen. IV*, II. 4. 145, 146: "I would I were a weaver; I could sing psalms."

64. *dog at*, clever at.   65. *lady*; the Virgin Mary.

68. *Thou knave*; this catch of two lines is found in a musical collection *Pammelia*, 1609. Like most *catches* (see G.), it has a comic effect, the parts being so distributed that each singer should call the other "knave" in turn.

80. *a Cataian*; a term of reproach, like "heathen Chinee"; see G.

81. *Peg-a-Ramsey*; the title of an Elizabethan song, only the tune of which is extant. If we knew the words, we might see the point of Sir Toby's remark, unless it is intentional nonsense. See p. 135.

"*Three merry men be we*"; the refrain or 'burden' of several old ballads; it is often quoted in Elizabethan plays. *be*, see G.

83. *Tilly-vally*, stuff! nonsense! See G. *lady!* a satirical echo of "my *lady*" in Maria's speech; it suggests to Sir Toby the line of the song in which "lady, lady" occurs. This song was *The Constancy of Susanna*, of which Mercutio sings this scrap in *Romeo and Juliet*, II. 4. 151. There were many old ballads about characters of the Old Testament and Apocrypha, e.g. "Jeptha, Judge of Israel" (*Hamlet*, II. 2).

91. "*O, the twelfth day*"; the beginning of a lost ballad; doubtless, it celebrated some battle or event that occurred on December 12. Old ballads often begin thus by mentioning the season in which the event described took place; cf. *The Boy and the Mantle*, in Percy's *Reliques*:

"In the third day of May,
    To Carleile did come."

94. *honesty*, decency, the sense of what is proper (=Lat. *honestas*).

95. *tinkers*; proverbial drinkers and talkers; cf. 1 *Henry IV*, II. 4. 19, 20, "I can *drink* with any *tinker* in his own *language*."

97, 98. *coziers*, cobblers; see G. *remorse*, pity, sparing.

101. *sneck* (or *snick*) *up!* a slang phrase = 'go and be hanged.'

102. *round*, plain-spoken: "be round with him!" *Hamlet*, III. 4. 5.

103. *harbours you*, shelters you, allows you to live here.

104. *allied*; a sort of quibble: 'though she is connected with you, she has no connection (i.e. no sympathy) with your disorderly ways.'

105. *separate yourself from*, i.e. give them up.

109. "*Farewell, dear heart*." This and the following lines printed as quotations are adapted from a ballad *Corydon's Farewell to Phillis*.

112. "*His eyes do show*." Possibly the Clown as he makes the quotation intends a sly allusion to Sir Toby's intoxicated state. Cf. v. 205 ("his eyes were set").

114. *Is't even so*, is it possible that you can misbehave so?

122. *Out o' tune, sir*. Said to Malvolio, in reference to his sneers at their singing, more especially at its want of melody (cf. "ye squeak"). Many editors substitute *time* for *tune*; cf. Malvolio's "no respect of *time* in you" (99), and Sir Toby's "We did keep *time*" (100). But the change is not necessary:

indeed, it makes almost too subtle a point, seeing that the knight is half-intoxicated and would not be likely to remember what exactly Malvolio had said. He only recollects in a vague way that their singing had been spoken of contemptuously.

124. *cakes and ale*, jollity, revelling; suggesting then the Church feast-days and public holidays, so disliked by Puritans. See p. 135.

126. *Saint Anne.* The mother of the Virgin Mary. He swears by a Saint to annoy the Puritan (152) Malvolio. Puritans much disliked the invocation of Saints as savouring of Roman Catholicism.

ginger; used to spice ale with.

129. In Elizabethan households the steward wore a chain of gold or silver as a badge of office; it was usually cleaned with bread-crumbs.

132. *rule*, according to most editors, 'conduct, behaviour'; see G.

134. *go shake your ears*; a common expression of contempt.

136. *challenge him the field*, i.e. *to* a duel. *field* = combat.

145. *gull him*, fool him; the gull was thought to be a stupid bird.

146. *nayword*, byword; see G. *recreation*, laughing-stock.

149. *possess us*, inform us.

152. *puritan*; with Shakespeare never a flattering term.

160. *time-pleaser*, time-server, one who suits his principles to his interests, e.g. by pleasing the powers that be (in this case Olivia).

affectioned, affected; see p. 152.

161. *cons state*; some explain 'studies a dignified deportment,' but this hardly suits "utters." I think that the reference is to Malvolio's pompous conversation; he learns up "arguments of *state*" (II. 5. 163) and brings forth fine, carefully studied sentences on state-affairs. See p. 136.

162. *swarths*, i.e. *swaths*; literally rows of mown grass. Here a figurative expression = 'by the yard' (in colloquial English).

the best persuaded, with the highest opinion of himself.

164. *his grounds of faith*, his firm belief; some read *ground*.

165. *that vice*, that flaw, weakness, i.e. Malvolio's vanity

169. *some epistles*; contrast the letter in II. 5. Perhaps Maria got afraid lest she should offend Olivia, who respected Malvolio much. She writes, as we shall see, a letter which is so vague that she could pretend (if necessary) that it did not refer to Malvolio. No doubt, she was jealous of his influence with Olivia.

173. *feelingly personated*, accurately portrayed.

174. *on a forgotten matter*, when the writing relates to something that happened long since.

184. *Ass, I doubt not*; perhaps punning on "*As* I doubt not." The quibble on *ass* and *as* occurs in *Hamlet*, v. 2. 43.

188. *will work with him*, i.e. take effect on; cf. II. 5. 215.

190. *his construction of it*, how he *construes*, i.e. interprets, it; cf. III. 1. 126.

193. *Penthesilea*; queen of the Amazons, a race (in classical mythology) of female warriors; here a title of admiration, applied humorously to the diminutive Maria (cf. "giant," I. 5. 218).

194. *Before me*, by my soul; this use of *before* arose from the expletive *before God!*

195. *beagle*, a small kind of hound.

201. *I am...out*; cf. our slang phrase 'out of it': i.e. if he spends his money and does not win ("recover") Olivia.

203. *call me cut*, call me a fool; a common phrase.

206. *Burnt sack* was wine heated or 'mulled.' *Sack*, see G.

Scene IV.

A delightful feature in *Twelfth Night* is the happy union of comedy and romance: we pass so easily from the one to the other. Here for instance how effective is the transition from the rollicking geniality of Sir Toby and his boon companions to the romance and gentle sentiment of Orsino and his court. The contrast between Scenes 3 and 4 heightens the effectiveness of each.

1. Cf. the beginning of the first Scene of the play. The time of action is evidently the morning ("good morrow, friends").

2. *but*, just, i.e. let me hear just.

3. Scan *ántique*, as always in Shakespeare; = 'old-fashioned.'

4. *passion*, feeling, i.e. of love.

5. *recollected* = carefully culled and so 'studied.' Orsino contrasts the artificial language ("terms") of present songs with the simple style of this "antique" ballad.

11. *Feste, the jester*. It seems a little odd that the Clown should be so much at Orsino's palace. But we saw in Act I (Sc. 5) that he absented himself often; probably Olivia's house was rather dull (despite Sir Toby), what with her mourning and Malvolio's fault-finding.

18. *motions*, emotions; cf. 101.

21. *to the seat*, i.e. to the heart; cf. I. 1. 37, 38.

25. *stayed upon*, rested on lingeringly. *favour*, face; see G.

26. *by your favour*. A quibble on the two senses (1) 'with your good pleasure,' (2) 'on your face' (*by* = 'near,' its original sense).

27. *complexion*, appearance, looks; not merely 'colour of the face.'

30, 31. Perhaps Shakespeare was thinking of his own case. Anne Hathaway whom he married was his senior by several years.

31. *wears to him*; as a garment gets to fit its wearer.

32. *sways level*; as a balance maintains its equilibrium; she does not descend in her husband's affection—keeps a steady place in it.

33–36. Contrast 98–106.

34. *fancies*, loves, as in I. 1. 14.

35. *worn*, i.e. worn out; *won* is a needless change.

38. *hold the bent*; as a bent bow keeps the same strain.

42–49. An allusion to marriage. *spinsters*; in its literal sense 'spinners.' *free*; happy, careless. *bones*, bobbins made of bone; a bobbin is a pin on which thread is wound. Katherine of Arragon is said to have introduced pillow-lace making ("bone lace") in Bedfordshire. *silly sooth*, plain, simple truth. *sooth*; see G. *old age*, "the ages past, the times of simplicity."

52. *Come away*, come here, come to me.

53. *Cypress*; either (1) a shroud made of the crape-stuff called *cypress* (see G.), or (2) a coffin of cypress-wood. Probably (2) is right, because the shroud is mentioned just after, and it was white, whereas this crape was usually black. Cypress-wood (which is very dark—cf. "black" in 61) was used for coffins; to which it was customary to tie bunches of yew and rosemary.

69. *There's for thy pains*; Orsino gives him money.

72. *paid*, i.e. paid for, suffered for.

74. *Give me leave*; a polite and playful way of dismissing the Clown by reversing their relative positions.

75. *the melancholy god*, i.e. Saturn; cf. *saturnine*, 'morose.'

77. *taffeta*, shot silk, the hue of which varies with the light; hence a symbol of changeableness, as is the *opal*, a stone that reflects different colours. The Clown thinks that Orsino's outward garb should harmonise with his changeable character.

80. *intent*, direction, aim. *be everywhere*, i.e. constantly change.

83. *cruelty*; see I. 5. 307.

86. *parts*, endowments of wealth, position etc.

87. *hold*, value. *as giddily*, as lightly.

88, 89. i.e. it is her beautiful person, form, that attracts me. *pranks*, adorns; see G. *attracts*, i.e. *that* attracts.

92. Note from this point to the end of the Scene the touches of that "irony" mentioned on p. 86—how Viola's remarks and Orsino's have for the audience a significance that is hidden from Orsino.

95. *be answer'd*, i.e. acquiesce in that answer.

96. *There is...sides.* A singular verb *preceding* a plural subject is common in Shakespeare, especially with the phrase 'There is.' Cf. *Cymbeline*, IV. 2. 371, "*There is* no more such *masters*." Coming first, before the plural subject has been mentioned, the singular verb appears less unnatural.

97. *Can*, i.e. *which* can.

99. *to hold*, i.e. *as* to hold; Shakespeare often omits *as* after *so*. Cf. *Macbeth*, II. 3. 55, "I'll make so bold to call."

retention, capacity to keep.

100–104. Observe how the same metaphor is carried through the passage—"appetite," "palate," "surfeit," "cloyment," "hungry," "digest." One of the great distinctions between Shakespeare's early and later styles is his use of metaphor. In the early plays he will often take a single metaphor and keep to it; in his later plays, the outcome of a richer, completely developed imagination, he gives us variety of imagery, just touching perhaps on one metaphor, and then passing to another and yet another. A metaphor worked out in detail is apt to obscure or lose the original point of comparison.

101. *motion*, impulse. *liver*; see I. 1. 37, note. *but the palate*, i.e. but *of* the palate. Their love is mere taste for, not hungry desire of.

102. *That suffer*; the plural antecedent of *that* is contained in *their* = 'of those' (100); cf. I. 5. 305, note. *cloyment*, surfeit, satiety.

103. *as the sea*; cf. I. 1. 11.

104. *compare*, comparison; often in Shakespeare and Milton.

106. *owe*, feel towards; see G.

110. *loved*, i.e. *who* loved; see I. 5. 108, note.

113. *blank*; the metaphor of a sheet of paper not written on.

114. *a worm*, i.e. a canker; cf. Milton, *Lycidas*, 45, "As killing as the canker to the rose."

115. *damask*, rosy (see G.); "bud" suggested the idea of the rose.

116. *green...yellow*; indicating sickness and grief respectively.

117, 118. One often sees emblematical figures on tombstones. A figure of Patience, symbolising the patient resignation of those who have erected the monument, is a natural emblem. The words *smiling at grief* probably qualify *She*, not *Patience*, the sense being, as Boswell says: "While she was smiling at grief, her placid resignation made her look like Patience on a monument." *smiling at*; the notion of half submitting to a thing, half scorning it. A very similar comparison and personification of Patience occur in *Pericles*, V. 1. 139.

like Patience on a monument; one of the phrases in *Twelfth*

Night that have become proverbial; for others note "greatness thrust upon them" (II. 5. 158)—"the whirligig of time" (v. 385). Almost all Shakespeare's plays (especially *Hamlet*) have enriched our language with proverbial sayings.

120, 121. i.e. we make great professions of love, but lack the will to carry them out.

123. When she says, '*I*, your page-*boy*, am the only *daughter* left,' Orsino naturally concludes that the sister did die, and that Viola puts the fact in this indirect way so as to hide her grief. Viola misleads him without actually saying anything untrue.

124. *I know not*; said aside; she hopes that Sebastian was saved.

127. *give...place*, yield, withdraw. *denay*, denial; used (only here) for the rhyme. Cf. Spenser, *Faerie Queene*, VI. 11. 15, "That with great rage he stoutly doth *denay*" (rhyming with *lay* and *pay*).

SCENE V.

2. *a scruple of*, the least bit of.

6. *sheep-biter*; here ="a morose, surly and malicious fellow" (Schmidt); commonly a slang term for a thief. *come by*, receive; the notion is 'to come near' (*by*) a thing, and so attain it.

9. *bear-baiting*, the pastime of setting on dogs to bait or worry a bear tied to a stake (III. 1. 129, 130); much disliked by the Puritans, hence distasteful to Malvolio, "a kind of Puritan" (II. 3. 152). Scott describes it vividly in *Kenilworth*, xvii.

14. *pity of*, a bad thing for.

17. *my metal of India*, my little jewel, my girl of gold. Gold was proverbially associated with India; cf. Dekker's *Old Fortunatus* (1600), I. 1, "It's *gold* sure...an *Indian* mine." The 1st Folio, as often, prints *mettle*, a form of *metal*. The 2nd Folio has *nettle*, indicating perhaps that Maria would make Malvolio smart with annoyance.

23. *close!* hide yourselves!

26. *with tickling*. Country-bred boys know how easily trout are caught thus in the summer, when the water in small streams runs low.

Exit Maria. It is curious, I think, that Maria does not stop to see how her plan succeeds. Perhaps she has to attend Olivia.

Enter Malvolio. Note how Malvolio is precisely in the frame of mind which will make him fall an easy victim to the plot. He is thinking of Olivia (thus he merely says "she," and does not mention her name). Perhaps Olivia has just shown him some mark of favour. At any rate, he is musing on her partiality for him and thanking his fortune." And then, in this affected

mood, he finds the letter which confirms his delusions, even to
the extent of bidding him "touch *fortune's* fingers" (171).

To attribute thus a particular mood to a character in view of
what is coming is a common device of dramatists. Thus at the
beginning of *The Merchant of Venice* Antonio is sad. Nothing
in his circumstances accounts for his melancholy. This mood is
attributed to him merely as a means of foreshadowing the mis-
fortunes that impend. A dramatist naturally arranges the outset
of a scene in such a way as to give the best dramatic effect of
harmony or contrast with what follows.

28. *she*, i.e. Olivia. *affect me*, care for me.

36. *jets*, struts; see G. *advanced*, puffed up.

38. *'Slight*, an abbreviation of the oath *God's light*; oaths
naturally get curtailed—cf. *'slid*, III. 4. 427, *'sblood*.

45. *the Strachy*; the Strachy family (?). Most likely an allusion, then clear, to a lady of rank who had married a servant
—either in real life or in some popular play or novel (cf. v. 121,
note). None of the attempted explanations helps us much,
though there is ingenuity in the suggestion that *Strachy* is a
corruption of *Stratici* from Greek στρατηγός ('general'), then
(it is said) a title of magistrates and governors in many parts of
Italy: if this were so, the phrase would mean "the Governor's
widow," and the reference might be to some Italian novel in
which such a marriage as Malvolio describes had occurred.

"Yeoman of the wardrobe" was the title of one of the superior
servants in great Elizabethan households. *yeoman*, see G.

46. *Jezebel*; an absurd reproach to apply to a man; but
Sir Andrew is the speaker. Cf. Sir Toby's *firago* III. 4. 302.

47. *deeply in*; the metaphor of sinking deep into mud.

48. *blows him*, makes his swell with pride.

50. *state*, chair of state. Malvolio now sits down on some
garden-seat and enacts the imaginary scene with his "officers"
and "Toby." He pictures himself (the ex-servant) remaining
seated while Sir Toby (the knight) stands meekly in his presence
and receives the reprimand. About line 90 we must imagine
Malvolio to rise from his "state," stroll up and down, and
suddenly notice the letter (cf. 91 "What employment?" etc.).
So the Scene is commonly represented on the stage.

51. *stone-bow*, a cross-bow from which stones or bullets were
thrown. Cf. *The Book of Wisdom* v. 22, "hailstones full of
wrath shall be cast as out of a stone-bow."

54. *branched*, ornamented with designs of leaves and flowers;
cf. 'flowered' as applied to silks etc. designed with patterns of
flowers.

58. *the humour of state*, the air of a great personage.

59. *travel of regard*, i.e. after letting my look pass slowly from one to another. Cf. F. *regard*, look.

61. *my kinsman Toby*. His familiarity in dropping the 'Sir' and claim of kinship (through Olivia) cannot fail to rouse Sir Toby.

66. "Pocket-*watches* were brought from Germany into England about 1580"—Malone. See v. 166.

with my—some rich jewel. Probably he meant to say *chain* (II. 3. 129), but remembered that he would be a steward no longer.

71. *with cars*; we should say, 'with wild horses'; cf. *Two Gentlemen of Verona*, III. 1. 265, 266, "a team of horse shall not pluck that from me," i.e. his secret. Needless changes have been proposed, as *by th' ears*.

74. *control*, authority.

75. Cf. *Henry V*, IV. 7. 133, "*take him* [deal him] a box o' th' ear."

91. *employment*, business: 'what's to be done here?'

92. *woodcock*; like the gull, typical of stupidity because thought to have no brains, and easily caught with "springes." *gin*, snare; see G.

94. i.e. 'and may the god of humour inspire him to read the letter out.' Sir Toby and the others have not seen Maria's letter (which differs much from what she intended to write—cf. II. 3. 169, note).

96, 97. *C...P*. Note that neither occurs in the address of the letter as read out by Malvolio. It has been suggested that the direction ended with the words, "with *care present*" (a common Elizabethan direction on the outside of letters), and that Malvolio omitted them.

97. *in contempt of question*, without doubt.

100. *Why that?* with his usual slowness, Sir Andrew does not see that Malvolio refers to the letter which he is studying.

103. *Soft!* stay: just as he is going to break the seal he notices its *impressure* = impression, mark; cf. *expressure* II. 3. 171.

104. *Lucrece*; the Roman matron Lucretia (wife of Tarquinius Collatinus), whose story is told in Shakespeare's early poem *Lucrece*. Her head was a common device of ladies' seals. See v. 341.

106. *liver*; see I. 1. 37, note.

111. *numbers*, metre; see G.

114. *brock*, badger; then a frequent term of contempt.

116. i.e. a knife such as that with which Lucrece stabbed herself. Shakespeare almost always accents *Lúcrece*, as here.

119. *fustian*, nonsensical; see G.

123. *What dish!* what *a* dish! *she*, Maria.

124. *staniel*, kestrel; a species of falcon. The Folios have *stallion*; Hanmer corrected. A hawk *checks* "when she forsakes her proper game, and follows some other of inferior kind that crosses her in her flight." Cf. III. 1. 71. The number of hawking-terms which Shakespeare and other Elizabethans use shows how popular the sport was.

128. *formal capacity*, ordinary intelligence, average ability.

135. *Sowter*; name of a hound; properly 'a cobbler' (Lat. *sutor*).

cry, "give tongue," as a hound does when it finds the scent.

136. *though it be*. Probably the sense is that Malvolio will continue his efforts to interpret the lines, "though the cheat is so *gross* that any one else would find it out"—Malone. A less egotistical man would be put on his guard by the plainness of the whole scheme.

140. A "fault" (in hunter's language) is when the scent fails.

141. *no consonancy*, what follows does not agree.

142. *suffers under probation*, will not bear looking into, testing.

144. *O shall end*; i.e. at the end Malvolio will have cause to say *O!* when he suffers for his presumption.

151, 152. *simulation*, disguise, counterfeiting. *to crush this*; i.e. with a little straining, it might be made to fit my name.

153, 154. *every one...are*; the verb is 'attracted' to the plural *letters*. Note how important a part in syntax 'attraction' plays—that is, the influence of one word, through either its grammatical form or its sense, upon another word in the sentence. Cf. I. 5. 171, note.

155. *revolve*, consider.

156. *my stars*, my fortunes; cf. 184, and see I. 3. 142, note.

157. *born great*; the Folios have *become* here, but *born* III. 4. 45.

161. *slough*, the skin cast off by a snake.

162. *opposite*; as we say, 'contrary.' *a kinsman*, i.e. Sir Toby.

163. *tang*, ring with; *twang* (III. 4. 197) is another form. The sound *tang* suggests a loud, wearisome voice always at work.

164. *singularity*, affectation; a 'singular' person is often affected.

166. *yellow stockings*; much worn in England in the 16th century. Most people know the light yellow hose worn by the Blue-Coat boys, the style of whose school-dress has not been altered since the foundation of Christ's Hospital in 1553.

167. *cross-garter'd*; also an Elizabethan fashion. Steevens believes that it was especially popular with Puritans: if so, it would be appropriate to Malvolio (II. 3. 152). See p. 136.

172. *alter*, exchange (i.e. instead of his being her servant).

173. *daylight and champain*, "broad day and an open country cannot make things plainer"—Warburton. *champain*, see G.

discovers; the two subjects really convey *one* idea, 'openness.'

176. *point-devise*, exactly (see G.), i.e. as the letter described.

178. *jade me*, make a fool of me.

180. *She did commend.* We must suppose that Olivia did so to please Malvolio, and that Maria heard her, for really she disliked the colour and the fashion (cf. Maria's words 218–220). Or perhaps Malvolio imagines it all, being "in such a dream" (211).

184. *strange*, reserved, distant in manner; cf. IV. I. 16.

185. *stout*, proud; cf. 2 *Henry VI*, I. I. 187, "stout and proud."

185, 186. *in yellow stockings...even with the swiftness of putting on.* In the earlier Scenes of *Twelfth Night* (as commonly represented) Malvolio is dressed entirely in black, which harmonises with his austere, somewhat Puritanical character, and increases by force of contrast the absurdity of his guise when he next appears (III. 4).

189. *entertainest*, art willing to accept.

let it appear in thy smiling. This point struck the barrister John Manningham when he saw *Twelfth Night* acted in 1602 (see *Introduction*). In the representation of the play the incident may be made very amusing both here where Malvolio begins to practise "smiling," and more in III. 4 when he comes into Olivia's presence.

198. *Sophy*, the Shah of Persia; see G. In 1598 an English embassy under Sir Robert Shirley (the most illustrious perhaps of Elizabethan travellers) and his brother Sir Anthony reached Persia. Sir Robert stayed till 1607, but Sir Anthony returned to England in 1599. The embassy was the first sent out from this country to Persia and roused great interest; much was said about the splendour of the Persian Court and the liberality of the Shah. Shakespeare's audience would see his allusion at once. So in *King Lear*, III. 6. 85 ("Persian attire").

199. *I could marry*; see v. 370–372.

208. *play*, stake. *tray-trip*, "a game at dice, in which success depended upon throwing a *trois*" (i.e. a *trey* or three); perhaps like backgammon.

215. *aqua-vitæ*, ardent spirits, e.g. brandy. So the Irish *usquebaugh* = 'whiskey' means 'water of life.'

225. *Tartar*, Tartarus, a classical name of the infernal regions.

ACT III.

SCENE I.

The time of this Scene is the same morning as in the last. Viola is on her way to Olivia, as Orsino directed (II. 4. 83, 125–127).

1. *Save thee*, i.e. God save thee; cf. III. 4. 238.

2. *tabor*, a small drum used by clowns and jesters.

3. He quibbles on *by* = 'by means of' and 'close by, near.'

4. *churchman*, clergyman.

8. *the king lies*, i.e. dwells, a common use of *lie*.

12. *You have said*; a form of assent = 'well said, quite right'; generally, as here, ironical; cf. *Othello*, IV. 2. 204.

To see this age! how clever the world is nowadays!

13. *cheveril*, of kid leather; see G. A clever man can twist a remark into just the opposite sense to what was intended.

17. *dally nicely*, trifle in a subtle manner.

25. *since bonds* etc.; see p. 136 and *Introduction*, p. ix.

39. *pilchards*; small fish like herrings.

41. *corrupter of words*, punster, maker of word-plays.

42. *I saw thee late*; i.e. when the Clown sang the Song, "Come away, come away, death" (II. 4. 52).

43. *the orb*, the earth.

45. *sorry but*, i.e. sorry if not. Cf. 2 *Henry IV*, IV. 3. 33, "I would be sorry *but* it should be thus" = *if* it were *not* thus.

48. *pass upon me*, make sallies of wit at my expense; the metaphor is from fencing; see III. 4. 302.

49. *there's expenses*; giving him a present (drinking-money).

52. *sick for one*; alluding to her love of Orsino.

55. *a pair of these*. He looks at the coin which Viola has given him and hints that he would like another. Similarly he gets a double 'tip' out of Orsino (V. 1.).

57. *put to use*, put out to interest. Cf. *Venus and Adonis*, 768, "But gold that's put to use more gold begets."

58. *Pandarus*, Cressida's uncle, who enabled the lovers Troilus and Cressida to meet. Their story was so popular in the Middle Ages that they became proverbial characters, Cressida as the faithless woman, Troilus as the faithful lover. It forms the subject of one of Chaucer's poems and one of Shakespeare's plays.

61, 62. *The matter...is not great*; 'it is not much to beg for a Cressida, seeing that she herself was but a beggar.' It was a tradition, mentioned by Chaucer in his *Troylus and Chryseyde*, that Cressida became "a beggar."

63. *construe*, explain.

65. *welkin*, sky (see G.); *element*, though it here means 'sphere,' sometimes meant 'sky' (cf. I. I. 26): hence the Clown humorously treats *element* and *welkin* as the same in sense, and interchanges them.

Perhaps *element* = 'sphere,' as in Malvolio's "I am not of your *element*" (III. 4. 137), was a piece of Elizabethan slang. Certain words and phrases become fashionable for a time, and *element* may have been much in vogue just when *Twelfth Night* was written. In comedy there are these touches of contemporary allusion—references, which soon lose their point, to things of the passing hour.

67–74. These lines are a good summary of the duties and qualifications of the professional Fool or Clown.

69. *their mood*, the mood of those; see I. 5. 305, note. The Fool must suit his fooling to different people and occasions.

71, 72. Just as the untrained hawk ("haggard") flies after *every* bird that crosses its flight, so the Fool must seize on *every* chance incident and make it an occasion of fooling. His duty, in short, is (1) to let slip no incident, (2) to treat the incident when he has seized it in a way that suits the persons and the circumstances. Especially in this latter point does the really competent Fool show his discrimination.

Many editors print "*Not*, like the haggard," arguing that a *trained* Fool such as the passage describes would not be compared with an *untrained* hawk. But (1) the comparison is limited to *one* point, viz. that the clever Fool, like the "haggard," catches at everything which "comes before his eye": this is the sole resemblance between them suggested, and it furnishes a just point of comparison. (2) The change of text, *not* for *and*, is too great. *haggard*; see G. and cf. the *Religio Medici*, I. x.: "I teach my *haggard* and unreclaimed reason to *stoop* unto the *lure* of faith." *checks*; see II. 5. 124, note.

74, 75. It is quite proper ("fit") that a Fool should "play the fool"—(67) that is "wisely": but wise men must not.

75. The 1st Folio reads "But *wisemens* folly falne, quite taint their wit." The reading in our text is the nearest to the Folio and that generally adopted. I suppose that the *s* in "wise men-*s*" was due to "wise man's" in 73, the printer repeating *s* by a mere slip.

folly-fallen, fallen into folly, grown foolish. *taint their wit*, infect their whole intelligence with folly and so spoil it; cf. III. 4. 14.

82, 83. *encounter*, go towards. *trade*, business. Shakespeare's satire of the affected diction of "courtiers" (97) is emphatic; cf.

Osric in *Hamlet*, the "Gentlemen" in *Winter's Tale*, v. 2. To "parley Euphuism" was quite the correct thing at Elizabeth's court.

86. *list*, end, goal; lit. 'boundary'; cf. *lists* of a tournament.

87. *taste*, make trial of (cf. III. 4. 267); another affected word.

89. Cf. *Two Gentlemen of Verona*, II. 5. 28: "*I understand* thee not"..."My staff *understands* me." Milton borrows the joke, *Paradise Lost*, VI. 625–627.

93. *gait*; with a quibble, I suppose, on *gate*; cf. "entrance."

94. *prevented*, anticipated; see G.

100. *pregnant*, ready. *vouchsafed*, graciously attentive.

102. *all ready*, i.e. for the first opportunity of using them. The 1st Folio has *already*.

110. *lowly feigning*, feigned lowliness, pretended humility.

114. *For him*, as for, as regards, him.

115. *blanks*; cf. II. 4. 113.

117. *by your leave*, excuse me; an apology for interrupting.

119. i.e. make love to her on his own (Cesario's) behalf.

120. *hear you to solicit*; see I. 5. 315, 317, note.

121. An allusion to the doctrine of Pythagoras that the eight (in later times, the number was raised to nine) "spheres" containing the planets and stars produced by their revolutions a music which is inaudible to mortal ears. Each sphere was thought to produce "one note in one tone"; and from all the eight notes there results a single harmony" (Plato's *Republic*, bk. x. 617). The notion of this "sphere-music" became proverbial and is often referred to in poetry. The theory of the "spheres" belonged to the Ptolemaic astronomy, the system adopted in *Paradise Lost*; see *Appendix* thereon in the Pitt Press editions of *Paradise Lost*.

122. *beseech*; Shakespeare often omits *I* with this word; see *The Tempest*, I. 2. 473. Cf. *prithee* short for "*I* pray thee."

123. i.e. "after the enchantment your presence worked in my affections" (Warburton). *here*; misspelt *heare* in the Folios.

124. *abuse*; probably = 'deceive'; see G.

126, 127. *hard construction*, unfavourable interpretation of my conduct; cf. II. 3. 190. *to force*, by forcing; cf. II. 5. 6.

128. *none of yours*; for *none* = 'nothing,' see I. 3. 113, note. *what might you think?* what could you think? Cf. I. 1. 24.

130. The metaphor of tying an animal to a stake and then setting on dogs to bait or worry it; cf. II. 5. 9, *Macbeth*, V. 7. 2, 3.

131, 132. i.e. to one who is so quick of perception ("receiving") as you are I have said enough to reveal my secret.

132. *cyprus*, a kerchief of crape; see G. *bosom*, the part of the body *and dress* concealing the *heart* = the actual "seat" of love.

Olivia means that Cesario (Viola) can see right into her heart and perceive the love that it cherishes for Cesario.

133. The voice rests on *hides*, making it metrically = two syllables; the later Folios insert *poor* before *heart*. Some editors read *hideth*.

134. *degree*, a step; for this literal use cf. *Julius Cæsar*, II. 1. 26, where Shakespeare speaks of the "degrees" of a ladder.

135. *grize*, a step; see G.

a vulgar proof, a common experience.

144. *proper*, fine, handsome; cf. II. 2. 30, note.

146. *Westward-ho!* and *Eastward-ho!* were cries ("up" and "down") of the boatmen on the Thames, the great medium of transport. Each served as the title of a comedy of London life. *Westward-ho!* also became associated with the Spanish Main; cf. Kingsley's book.

151, 152. Apparently Viola means that Olivia forgets her position—"what she is"—in declaring her love for a page. Olivia replies that she *does* forget her position and Cesario's (Viola's) too.

160. *would seem hid*, wishes to remain hidden.

163. *maugre*, in spite of (F. *malgré*).

165, 166. *Do not extort* etc.; 'do not, from what I have just said ("this clause"), force reasons, on your part ("thy"), for thinking that because I woo you, *you* have no cause to woo (or "love") me.' The need of rhyme causes some ambiguity of expression, as often.

167. *thus*, with this thought, viz. that "Love sought" etc.

171. *that*, her love, which is implied by "heart, bosom, truth." *nor never*, emphatic negative; cf. II. 1. 1.

172. *save I*; see *save* in G.

Scene II.

6. *I saw your niece*; he alludes to the meeting of Olivia and Cesario (Viola) in the last Scene; cf. his letter III. 4. 171.

8. *orchard*, garden, i.e. of Olivia's house; see G.

9. *the while*, in the meantime; *while* was originally a noun meaning 'time'—cf. v. 414.

12. *argument*, proof; so *argue* = to prove (Lat. *arguere*), cf. *Paradise Lost*, IV. 830, "Not to know me argues yourselves unknown."

22. *liver*; here regarded as the seat of courage; cf. 66.

23. *accosted*; cf. I. 3. 52, and see G.

fire-new from the mint, i.e. just coined.

26. *looked for*, expected of you. *balked*, neglected, omitted.

28. *sailed into the north*; you are regarded coldly by her.

29. *like an icicle*... This has been thought to allude to the discovery of Northern Nova Zembla in 1596 by Barents, a Dutchman. The ruins of the house he built there were discovered in 1871 (*Shakespeare's England*, I. 181).

34. *had as lief*, would as willingly; cf. Germ. *lieber*, rather, sooner.

The *Brownists* were a Puritan sect, so called from their leader Robert *Browne*, a noted Separatist or Independent in Elizabeth's reign. They seem to have been "the constant objects of popular satire" in Shakespeare's time (Steevens).

politician; in Shakespeare a depreciatory word = 'schemer, intriguer.'

35. *Build me; me* is the indirect object = '*for* me.' This datival use of the pronoun is common in Shakespeare, and illustrates the *inflected* element in English (see p. 155). Cf. "challenge *me*" (36), "bear *me*" (43), "make *me*" (I. 5. 287), "hear *me* this" (v. 123).

38–41. *assure thyself*; 'be sure that nothing recommends a man more to a woman than a reputation for courage.' *broker*, agent.

46. *curst*, sharp in your language; see G. *it is no matter how*, you need not trouble to be witty.

48. *if thou thou'st*; to address anyone with whom you were not intimate as *thou* was a mark of great contempt; cf. *tutoyer* in French.

51. *the bed of Ware*; the famous oak bedstead, about 11 feet square and 7½ feet high, able to hold 12 persons, which was long at the "Saracen's Head" Inn at Ware, in Hertfordshire. It is still preserved.

52. *gall*, bitterness, rancour; also, ox-gall was then used in ink.

56. *cubiculo*, chamber; an Italian form from Lat. *cubiculum*.

57. *a dear manakin to you*; for the position of *dear*, on which *to you* depends, cf. *Richard II*, III. 1. 9, "A *happy* gentleman *in blood* and lineaments," i.e. happy in blood, etc. Such transpositions are common in Shakespeare. (Abbott, pp. 308, 309.)

58. *dear to him*; expensive (having borrowed so much money).

64. *wainropes*, cart-ropes. *hale*, drag.

65. *if he were, and you find*; in Shakespeare, as in ordinary *spoken* English, strict sequence of tenses is often neglected.

66. A "white," bloodless liver was thought a mark of cowardice.

67. *anatomy*, body (said with contempt); properly 'skeleton.'

68. *opposite*, opponent, adversary; cf. III. 4. 253, 293.

70, 71. "The wren generally lays nine or ten eggs at a time, and the last hatched of all birds are usually the smallest and weakest of the whole brood." Maria's smallness was alluded to in I. 5. 218.

nine; a correction of the reading *mine* of the Folios.

72. *the spleen*, 'a fit.'

74, 75. Probably an echo of the Prayer-Book (Athanasian Creed).

renegado, apostate, i.e. no longer a Christian; see G.

77. *impossible passages of grossness*, incredible acts of stupidity; cf. *Much Ado*, v. I. 164. Some interpret 'gross impositions.'

80. *pedant*, schoolmaster, pedagogue; so always in Shakespeare.

81. The practice of holding school in a church, or in a room over the porch, was not uncommon. Shakespeare must have seen the boys going to school at St Olave's by the Bankside, near the Globe Theatre, or St Michael's, Cornhill. During his boyhood the grammar school at Stratford was held in the old Chapel of the Guild (*Shakespeare's England*, I. 227).

85. A time reference for the date of *Twelfth Night*. The "new map" was a map of the world published in 1600, which created a great stir because of its "lines," i.e. rhumb-lines = "a set of straight lines drawn through a point on a map or chart to indicate the course of a ship sailing continuously in any direction." *It was our first scientific map*, and was drawn by a Cambridge mathematician, Edward Wright, the pioneer of nautical science. It is reproduced in *Shakespeare's England*, I. 174, and the student who is able to consult that invaluable work will appreciate the point of Maria's simile. The treatment too of India and the East is fuller and more accurate than in any previous map: hence "augmentation." The fact that the great trading society, the East India Company, the foundation of our empire in India, received its charter from Queen Elizabeth in 1600 gives additional interest to references like this and the earlier one (II. 5. 17).

Scene III.

That all the events of the play from this point to the end take place on the same day is proved by v. 96, 97.

2. i.e. since the trouble ("pains") of following me pleases you.

6. 'And it was not *only* love that did incite ("spur") me.'

8. *jealousy*, anxiety, fear.

9. *Being skilless in*, since you are a stranger in.

13. Scan "my kínd | Antón|io," slurring the last two letters of the name into *one* extra syllable. Long proper names at the end of a line often bear only one accent and get slurred (i.e. shortened) thus.

15, 16. 'And often the obligation of kindnesses is got rid of with such valueless pay.' *shuffled off*; the metaphor of getting free from a fetter or chain; cf. *Hamlet*, III. 1. 67, "When we have shuffled off this mortal coil."

17. *my worth*, what I am worth, i.e. my wealth.

19. *reliques*, monuments, i.e. old buildings, etc.

26. *in a sea-fight*; see v. 54–66. *the count his*; see *his* in G. S. rightly limits the galley, a long oared vessel, to the Mediterranean; it was obviously unsuitable for rough northern waters.

29. *Belike*, I suppose, probably; =*by likelihood*.

32. *bloody argument*, cause of bloodshed.

34. *for traffic's sake*, on account of our trade.

36. *lapsed*, caught, found. The word properly means 'fallen'; here the context implies 'fallen into a trap,' i.e. caught.

39. *In the south suburbs*; he chooses an inn away from the busy part of the town as being safer for him. "Elephant" is not an uncommon name for an inn; cf. the well-known "Elephant and Castle." Shakespeare refers here to a London tavern close to the Globe Theatre on the Bankside (which was outside the bounds of the "City"—hence "suburbs"—on the *south* bank of the Thames). A merchant of Ragusa, whose letters from London (1590–1591) to a friend in Florence have been discovered recently, mentions that an Italian acquaintance was lodging at "the Elephant." In *The Taming of the Shrew*, IV. 4. 4, 5, S. transfers to Genoa a London tavern, the Pegasus in Cheapside, mentioned in other Elizabethan plays. (*The Times Literary Supplement*, July 10, August 21, 1919; *Shakespeare's England*, II. 174, 175.)

44. *toy*, trifle; see G.

45, 46. *store*, possessions. *not for*, not suitable for, i.e. you have no money to waste. *idle markets*, unnecessary purchases.

Scene IV.

As regards the time of action, this Scene follows immediately on the last. Thus between Antonio's giving his purse to Sebastian and asking for it back (see lines 368–386 of this Scene) "not half an hour" elapsed (v. 95).

The Scene is laid in the garden so that Sir Toby and the others may look on without being seen. Maria had promised them a good view.

1. *him*, Cesario (Viola). *he says*, suppose that he says.

2. *bestow of*, i.e. *on*. Elizabethan writers often use *of* = *on* and *on* = *of*; cf. *Merry Wives of Windsor*, I. 4. 80, "he came *of* an errand."

5. *sad*, sober, grave; see G. *civil*, well-mannered.

9. *possessed*, i.e. with an evil spirit, so 'mad.'

12. *you were best*; see I. 5. 34.

14. *tainted*; cf. III. 1. 75, note.

20. *upon a sad occasion*, on a serious matter; Malvolio takes *sad* in its common sense 'sorrowful.'

25. "*Please one and please all.*" A ballad with this title, thought to have been written by Richard Tarleton, Queen Elizabeth's jester, is extant. For *sonnet* = 'poem,' see G.

30, 31. *Roman hand*. An allusion to the elegant "Italian" style of handwriting which came into fashion in England in the Elizabethan age. See *Shakespeare's England*, I. 201.

38. *daws* (jackdaws), so called from the noise they make.

40. *this boldness*. Maria artfully uses a word which makes him quote the advice in the letter, "be not *afraid*."

52–61. Of course, Olivia, not knowing that Malvolio quotes the words of the letter in which *thy...thee* referred to him, thinks that by *thy* and *thee* Malvolio means her. Cf. her exclamation "Am *I* made?"

54. *Thy yellow stockings!* In her amazement she repeats his words; but she means *my*.

59. *Am I made?* are my fortunes made? A ridiculous thing for a servant to tell his high-born, wealthy mistress.

61. *midsummer madness*; a proverbial phrase. It was supposed that at Midsummer, "the brain, being heated by the intensity of the sun's rays, was more susceptible of those flights of imagination which border on insanity, than at any other period of the year" (Drake). By using such a strong phrase Olivia perhaps means that Malvolio is in a worse state than Maria led her to anticipate (8–14).

67–70. *Let this fellow...my dowry*. Important as showing the high esteem in which Olivia holds Malvolio, and which we must not ignore. The difficulty of acting the part of Malvolio is to preserve respect for his merits, yet bring out the ludicrousness of the mistake, and of the situations, into which his great failing (vanity) betrays him. Some editors think that Olivia refers here to Cesario. *miscarry*, come to harm.

80, 81. *sad*; cf. 5. *in the habit*, with the bearing of a great man.

82. *limed her*, caught her, as a *bird* with birdlime.

83. *Jove's...Jove*. Some believe that Shakespeare wrote *God's...God* (which Halliwell even prints), and that the editors of the 1st Folio made the change because of the statute of James I. forbidding profanity on the stage. There are cases where this happened; but surely the reading here ought to correspond with II. 5. 107 ("*Jove* knows I love") and 184 ("*Jove* and my stars"), and, considering the ludicrous character of all three

passages, I doubt very much whether Shakespeare would have introduced the name *God* into them.

84. *Fellow*; he thinks that Olivia (67) used *fellow* = 'companion' or 'equal'; whereas she meant 'this man' (said with some contempt).

85. *after my degree*, i.e. according to (Lat. *secundum*) my rank.

86, 87. A quibble on *scruple* = (1) 'a doubt,' (2) 'the third part of a dram,' i.e. a very small amount.

88. *incredulous*, incredible.

95. *drawn in little*, compressed into a small space.

Legion; "Treated as a noun proper, to denote a compound of all the devils of hell" (Schmidt). See *Mark* v. 9, *Luke* viii. 30.

98. *man*; a familiar form of address, which, coming from the servant Fabian, vexes Malvolio (as it was meant to).

99. *Go off*. Note how Malvolio now puts into practice the advice of the letter—"be opposite...surly" etc.

100. *private*, privacy; cf. "in *private*."

108. *he's an enemy*; see II. 2. 29, note.

121. *move him*, make him angry.

125. *my bawcock*, my fine fellow; see G.

128. *Biddy*; a kind of nonsense word used by children in calling chickens (cf. "chuck") to feed. Perhaps this is from some ballad.

129. *cherry-pit*; a childish game of pitching cherry-stones into a little hole.

130. *Collier*; then a term of abuse. "The devil is called a *Collier* for his blackness," says Johnson; he quotes the proverb, "'Like will to like,' quoth the Devil to the Collier." Scott gives another version: "Match for match, quoth the devil to the collier" (*Kenilworth*, xiv.).

142. *genius*, spirit = Lat. *genius* (Gk. δαίμων), 'a guardian, spirit.'

145. *taint*; just as something exposed to the air goes bad.

148. Shakespeare alludes several times to the practice of confining madmen in a dark house or room—a supposed cure for lunacy—and fettering them. Cf. *Comedy of Errors*, IV. 4. 95, 97:

"Mistress, both man and master is *possess'd*;
They must be *bound* and laid *in some dark room*."

150. *carry it*, manage it, i.e. their plan.

154. *finder*, discoverer; but there is an allusion (cf. "bar") to the legal phrase 'to *find*,' as in '*find* guilty' = 'bring in a verdict of guilty.'

156. *May morning*; an allusion to the festivities formerly held on May 1st, such as 'going a-Maying,' i.e. to gather hawthorn, crowning the May-Queen, setting up the May-pole, singing May-carols, etc.

165. *admire*, be surprised; see G.

168. *note*, remark.

171. *in my sight*; see III. 2. 8, note.

174. *sense-less*; Sir Andrew is not to hear the last syllable.

181. Cf. *Much Ado About Nothing*, II. 1. 327, "it keeps on the windy side of care," i.e. the safe side. A metaphor taken from seamanship: when two sailing-boats race, that which is *to windward* has an advantage over the other. The reference cannot well be to sport: if you approach game "on the windy side" = the side *from* which the wind blows (the natural meaning), the scent is carried by the wind and the game startled; i.e. "the windy side" is the wrong one to choose.

184. *upon one of our souls*, i.e. the soul of the man killed in the duel; Sir Andrew hopes that it may not be *his* soul.

191. *commerce*, intercourse.

193. *scout me*, keep watch *for* me; cf. "build *me*," III. 2. 35, note.

194. *bum-baily*, a subordinate officer of the law, employed to execute sheriff's writs and (in former days) to arrest debtors. The word is exactly similar in sense and formation to F. *pousse-cul*.

195. *draw*, i.e. thy sword.

198. *gives manhood more approbation*, gains a man more credit for courage than an actual test of it would.

203. *gives him out to be*, shows him to be.

208. *clodpole*, blockhead.

215. *cockatrice*; a fabulous serpent, also called *basilisk*; the glance of its eyes was supposed to be deadly. Cf. *Romeo*, III. 2. 47, "death-darting eye of cockatrice."

217. *presently*, immediately, i.e. directly after Cesario leaves.

222. *laid...on't*. Probably = 'staked upon it,' from the metaphor of '*laying* a wager,' i.e. betting. Cf. 433 and *Hamlet*, V. 2. 174, "he hath *laid on* twelve *for* nine" (= 'twelve *to* nine'). The *it* ('*t*) refers to the whole idea in "I have said too much." For *on't* many would substitute *out*, taking *laid out* = 'exposed to reproach.' *unchary*, heedlessly.

228. *jewel*, trinket; probably a 'miniature' portrait set in gold and gems, which might well be called a 'jewel'; a favourite sort of gift. Miniature-painting reached a high pitch under the Tudors.

232. i.e. that may be given to you without loss of honour.

234. *with mine honour*; if she gives to Orsino the love which she has already given to Cesario (Viola), then her honour will not be "saved" (232)—she *will* have lost it.

238. *God save thee*; we had the French phrase, III. 1. 78. Note that Sir Toby, wishing to be familiar, says *thee*, and that Viola replies by the more formal *you*.   243. *attends*, awaits.

244. *dismount thy tuck*, draw thy sword; another of Sir Toby's affected phrases (used ironically to the "courtier"); like the affected Osric's use of "carriages" for the straps or "hangers" of a sword-belt (*Hamlet*, V. 2. 156–160). The Italian was the great school of fencing in Shakespeare's time. Italian masters taught fencing in London. Hence many fencing-terms, like *tuck* (see G.), were of Italian origin. *yare*, ready, quick; see G.

257, 258. Sir Toby wishes Cesario (Viola) to believe that Sir Andrew, though not a warrior with great military distinctions, is none the less a terrible fellow to deal with in private affairs of honour.

dubbed, knighted. *unhatched*, not hacked with blows; see G.

on carpet consideration, i.e. as a "*carpet*-knight." "*Carpet*-knights" were those who received knighthood in *consideration* of civil (not military) services to the state, or merely through the personal favour of the monarch. As they knelt to receive their honour, not on the field of battle but on the *carpeted* floor of some court-chamber, they were termed "*carpet*-knights." The distinction was thought little of compared with that of the knight who won his knighthood in time of war for brave exploits, and gradually "*carpet*-knight" came to be a contemptuous term for an effeminate, unwarlike man. So in *Much Ado About Nothing*, V. 2. 32, *carpet-monger* signifies one who is more at home on the *carpets* of ladies' bowers than on battle-fields.

260. *divorced*, separated (i.e. he has killed three men in duels).

261. *satisfaction can be none*; i.e. *there* can be; the omission of *there* is common.

The position of *none* = 'not at all' expresses emphasis. Cf. *Paradise Lost*, XI. 612, "but they his gifts acknowledged none."

262. *hob, nob*, hit or miss; come what may; see G.

265. *conduct*, escort; cf. the phrase 'safe conduct.'

266. *put quarrels on*, pick quarrels with.

267. *taste*, try, put to the proof; cf. III. 1. 87.

268. *quirk*, humour; see G.

269, 270. *derives itself*, springs from. *competent*, sufficient.

275. *meddle you must*, you cannot get out of the difficulty, you must do something (i.e. fight).

278. *know of*, ask; cf. *Othello*, V. 1. 117, "Go know of Cassio where he supp'd tonight."

280. *nothing of my purpose*, no intentional injury or insult.

286. *arbitrement*, decision; Fabian means 'a duel to the death.'

290. *Nothing of that...*, 'Judging by his outward appearance you would never suppose him to be the terrible fellow that in actual combat you will find him.'

298. *sir priest*; cf. "*Sir* Topas the curate" in IV. I, and "*Sir* Hugh Evans, a Welsh parson" in *The Merry Wives of Windsor*. The title *Sir* was formerly applied to clergymen because "*dominus*, the academical title of a Bachelor of Arts, was usually rendered by *Sir* in English at the Universities....Therefore, as most clerical persons had taken that first degree [namely, B.A.], it became usual to style them *Sir*."—Nares. The title *dominus* is still retained at Cambridge, being abbreviated in the official class-lists to *Ds*.

301. *Re-enter Sir Toby*. Dyce begins a new Scene here, and when *Twelfth Night* is acted there is commonly a slight change of scenery to shew that the rest of the Act takes place at "the orchard-end" (244), where Sir Andrew is waiting. The change is indicated (1) by Sir Toby's words (282) "till my return"; (2) by v. 67, where Antonio is described as having been arrested "in the streets." No doubt, the street or road running by the boundary of the "orchard," i.e. garden, is meant: Antonio coming along this street sees the confusion by the garden, takes part in it, and is arrested there. Neither he nor the Officers would be likely to have intruded into Olivia's private grounds. The change is not marked in the Folios, perhaps because it is not to an entirely different locality but only just to the end of the same garden in which the other events have taken place. It is convenient for references to retain the old arrangement.

302. *firago*, i.e. *virago*; properly applied to a shrewish woman. Cf. Sir Andrew's use of *Jezebel* (II. 5. 46) as a reproach for a man.

a pass, a bout; as we say, 'a turn with' the rapier. In fencing *pass* generally means 'thrust'; cf. III. 1. 48.

303. *the stuck*, the thrust; see G. Shakespeare is fond of fencing terms; cf. "answer," "bout," "motion" (the attack in fencing).

305. *answer*, the return thrust after parrying or receiving a hit.

307. *the Sophy*; cf. II. 5. 198 and see G.

316. *I'll make the motion*, I will propose it to him.

319. *ride you*; a slang phrase = 'make a fool of you.' He means to get Sir Andrew's horse for himself.

320. *to take up*, to make up, settle.

322. *as horribly conceited*, has an equally fearful opinion of him.

337. *by the duello*, according to the laws of duelling; see G.

343. *this young gentleman*; of course, Antonio mistakes Cesario (Viola) for Sebastian from whom he parted so recently (III. 3).

344. *Have done*; the subjunctive *have* puts the matter doubt-fully—'if it really is the case that.' Antonio does not think it likely that Sebastian has done wrong.

349. *undertaker*, meddler, one who undertakes another's business.

359. *This is the man.* Apparently the Officers have heard of Antonio's being in the town and have come in pursuit of him.

363. *favour*, face; cf. II. 4. 24.

366. *with seeking*, i.e. from; *with* often denotes a cause; cf. phrases like "pale with fear," "die with terror," *Lucrece*, 183, 231.

379. *having*, property, possessions. Cf. *Merry Wives of Windsor*, III. 2. 73, "the gentleman is of no *having*."

380. *my present*, the money which I have with me.

381. *now*, at such a time as this; said with emphasis.

382. *my deserts to*, my deserving acts towards, i.e. kindnesses.

383. *lack persuasion*, fail to move you.

385. *upbraid*, reproach—'cast in your teeth' (Lat. *objicere*).

397. *venerable*, worthy of respect. *did*, paid.

400–404. Antonio expresses to Viola the very sentiment that she expressed to the Captain (I. 2. 48–51): a fine touch of humour.

400. *feature*, general appearance, exterior; not a particular feature of the face (its modern use). Cf. *complexion* II. 4. 27; both words have narrowed in sense.

Of course, Antonio thinks that Cesario (Viola), whom he mistakes for Sebastian, disowns him because he is in trouble; cf. v. 90.

403. *the beauteous-evil*, those who are beautiful but bad; cf. "proper-false," II. 2. 30. "Whited sepulchres," as Scripture says.

404. *trunks o'erflourished*, chests carved with elaborate designs. In old country-houses one often sees such pieces of furniture. Cotgrave (1611) has "*Fringoteries*: Frets, wriggled *flourishings* in carving." Anyone who has ever done wood-carving will know exactly what Shakespeare seems to have meant by "o'erflourished." Some, however, think that the metaphor is from tree-trunks, decayed and hollow within but covered with verdure (moss, fungi, etc.) outside.

407, 408. 'His words seem to spring from such genuine feeling that he cannot be pretending.'

412, 413. *a couplet*, i.e. a couple. *saws*, maxims; see G.

415. *living in my glass.* She is so like Sebastian that when she looks in her mirror she, as it were, sees him. *living*, to be living.

417, 418. We have not been told previously that she was dressed like her brother—only that she had donned a page's dress. The similarity of dress had helped to mislead Antonio.

418. *if it prove*, if it turn out to be *so*, viz. that she has been mistaken for her brother (410).

419. *fresh in love*, full of love (kindness). In *fresh* applied to "*salt* waves" there is a quibble; cf. 'fresh (i.e. not salt) water.'

427. *'Slid*; short for the oath *God's lid*; see II. 5. 38, note.

431. *event*, issue, result; then a common meaning; cf. Lat. *eventus*.

432. *yet*, after all.

ACT IV.

SCENE I.

2. *sent for you*, i.e. by Olivia. The Clown supposes that he is speaking to Cesario (Viola), as in III. I (beginning of the Scene).

5. *well held out*, you are keeping up the pretence well (i.e. of not knowing the Clown).

6. *nor...not*; a good illustration of the double negative.

10. *vent*, 'utter.' In *As You Like It*, II. 7. 41, Jaques speaks of the Fool "venting" his nonsense. There may have been some contemporary joke about the word.

14, 15. *I am afraid...a cockney*. A common meaning of *cockney* (see G.) in Shakespeare's time was 'an effeminate, affected person.' That is the meaning here. The Clown thinks that Sebastian, for a man, talks in an effeminate, affected style; and he indicates his opinion by saying, 'I suppose affectation will soon be universal: that clumsy monster the world will be taking to an affected, mincing style of language and manner.' Viola had ridiculed the Clown himself somewhat for "dallying nicely with *words*" (III. I. 17): perhaps the Clown, mistaking Sebastian for Viola, intends his present remark as a retort.

16. *ungird*, relax. *strangeness*, reserved manner; cf. II. 5. 184.

19. *Greek*; then a colloquial term for a jovial, merry person. Cf. Minsheu (*Dictionary*, 1617), "a merie Greeke...a jester." The use arose from the Roman view of the Greeks as a genial, pleasure-loving people; cf. Lat. *græcari*, 'to live in the Greek (i.e. easy) manner.' So in "as merry as a *grig*," i.e. a *Greek*.

22. *open*, liberal; cf. 'open-handed'=generous. The Clown, of course, thinks that this is the second time that Cesario (Viola) has given him a present, the first time being in III. I. 49–60.

24. *after fourteen years' purchase*; a legal phrase connected with the buying of land. The ordinary price of land in Shakespeare's time was 12 years' purchase: hence by 14 years the Clown implies "a very extravagant price."

25. *met you again*; Sir Andrew had pursued Viola (III. 4. 427).

32. *tell my lady*. It seems rather mean in the Clown to tell

tales of his friends, but the play requires that he should let Olivia know, so that she may be brought upon the scene and thus meet Sebastian.

I would not be. He knows how angry Olivia will be with Sir Toby and Sir Andrew for assaulting Sebastian, whom he mistakes (as Olivia does afterwards) for Cesario (Viola).

36. *action*, law-suit; cf. v. 282. *battery*, unlawful assailing and striking; a legal phrase, more fully 'assault and battery.' Shakespeare uses legal terms frequently and with accuracy; and this has been considered by some to confirm the vague tradition that as a youth he was for a time in an attorney's office. Cf. 24, above, and 57 ("extent"): see also I. 3. 7; I. 5. 142, 143 (note), 263; III. 4. 154.

43. *well fleshed*; like a hawk or hound that has tasted the blood of its quarry (game), and been made fiercer thereby. Sebastian, to whom the words are addressed, has been "fleshed" upon Sir Andrew.

47. *malapert*, saucy. Sir Toby, unlike his friend, is brave.

52. In *Cymbeline*, IV. 2. 100, 120 *mountaineer* implies 'savage, barbarous'; so in Milton's *Comus*, 426, "No savage fierce...or mountaineer."

55. *Rudesby*, rough fellow; cf. *Taming of the Shrew*, III. 2. 10, "a mad-brain rudesby." Olivia addresses Sir Toby.

56. *sway*, rule.

57. *extent*, violent attack; a legal term; see G.

59. *fruitless*, idle, pointless.

60. *botch'd up*, made up, brought about; cf. I. 5. 51.

61. *thou shalt not choose but*, you must. Perhaps the full form of the expression would be 'thou shalt not choose *anything but* (i.e. except) *to* go.' Olivia must be pleased and surprised at "Cesario's" sudden complacency.

62. *Beshrew*, woe to! a plague upon! See G.

63. *Start*; a technical word for rousing game; cf. 1 *Henry IV*, I. 3. 198, "to *start* a hare." So there is probably a pun on *heart* and *hart* (stag), as in I. 1. 17, 18.

Scene II.

2. *Sir Topas*. The name is from Chaucer, *Sir Thopas* being the title of one of the *Canterbury Tales*. On *Sir* see III. 4. 298.

7. *not tall enough*; he has not an imposing presence such as would show off his clerical robes to the best effect.

10. *housekeeper*, host; cf. *housekeeping* = hospitality, or hospitable ways, 2 *Henry VI*, I. 1. 191. *goes as fairly*; 'it is just as honourable to be called ("said") an honest man as to be called a scholar.'

11. *careful*; full of the poor scholar's cares and wants.

12. *competitors*, confederates, partners; see G.

14. *Bonos dies*. The Clown attempts to talk Latin in his character as clergyman.

15. *the old hermit*; I imagine that this is one of the Clown's imaginary characters; see I. 5. 39, note.

16. *King Gorboduc*; an ancient British King. The name would be familiar to an Elizabethan audience since there was a well-known play, the earliest blank-verse tragedy in English, called *Gorboduc* (or *Ferrex and Porrex*), 1561.

21. *Peace!* the salutation of a clergyman on entering a house. Cf. the *Prayer-Book* ('Visitation of the Sick'), "Peace be to this house, and to all that dwell in it."

23. *Malvolio [Within]*. Note that throughout this scene Malvolio speaks from an inner chamber (the "dark room," III. 4. 148).

36. *modest*, moderate; he might have said something much more offensive than "*dishonest* Satan."

40, 41. *bay-windows* = *bow-windows*, which form a *bay* or *bow*, i.e. recess, in a room. Of course, there are no windows. *barricadoes*; see G.

clear-stories. The 1st Folio has *cleere stores*, commonly taken as a reference to the *clear-* (or *clere-*) *story* of Gothic architecture. See G., and cf. an extract in the *New English Dictionary* from an architectural work of the 17th century which speaks of "*Clear story, Bay windows*...and sundry other things in architecture" (T. Willsford's *Architectonice*, 1659). The other Folios have *cleare* (i.e transparent) *stones*: if that is the right reading, then it is intentional nonsense like the notion of "transparent" *barricadoes* or a "south-north" aspect.

43. *obstruction*, i.e. to the view.

48. *the Egyptians*. Exodus x. 21–23.

51–53. *abused*, ill-treated, used badly. *question*; perhaps 'discussion.' *constant*, consistent, logical.

54. *Pythagoras*, the Greek philosopher supposed to have first taught the doctrine of the transmigration of souls, e.g. that the souls of some human beings pass after their death into the forms of animals. The Clown asks the question because he knows that Malvolio, as a Puritan, will consider such a pagan idea very offensive.

63, 64. *allow of*, admit. "The Clown mentions a *woodcock* particularly, because that bird was supposed to have very little brains, and therefore was a proper ancestor for a man out of his wits"—Malone.

68. *for all waters*, ready for anything. Sir Toby has com-

plimented him on the skill with which he has played his part;
he replies, "O, I can assume any character—clergyman or clown:
I can turn my hand to anything." The metaphor is probably
that of a fish "which can swim equally well in all waters"—
Malone. Some think that the phrase refers to an Italian proverb,
meaning 'thou hast a cloak for all waters'; others, that *waters*
has a colloquial Elizabethan sense 'potations.'

75. *so far in offence*; through his encounter with Sebastian
(IV. I).

Exeunt. Maria does not appear again. It was apparently
after leaving the stage here with Sir Toby that she got married
(v. 372).

78. *Hey Robin.* This song, found in a MS. volume dating from
the reign of Henry VIII, is printed in Percy's *Reliques of Ancient
English Poetry.* It is a dialogue between two lovers, Robin and
his friend, who discuss their love-affairs in question and answer.

80. *Fool.* Malvolio first addresses the Clown in his usual con-
temptuous way, but soon becomes more courteous ("*Good* fool").
Contrast his tone towards the Clown in this Scene with that in
I. 5.

81. *perdy*; French *pardieu*, a common oath, corrupted.

87. *help me*; understand *so*, corresponding to '*as* ever thou
wilt' = 'in proportion as.'

89. *I will live to be thankful*; the emphasis is on *thankful*, not
live.

92. *how fell you besides?* how did you lose?

93. *five wits*; then a proverbial term by which "common wit,
imagination, fantasy, estimation, memory" were indicated. The
"five wits" corresponded to (sometimes were identified with)
the "five senses."

94. *notoriously*; as we say 'scandalously' i.e. shamefully.

96. *But as well?* only as well? The emphasis is on *but*.

99. *propertied me*, treated me as though I were a mere tool or
implement, not as a man with a will of my own. Cf. *King John*,
v. 2. 79, "I am too high-born to be *propertied*," and *Julius Cæsar*,
IV. I. 36, 40, "A barren-spirited fellow...a *property*," i.e. one
with whom you can do what you please. *Property* keeps the idea
'implement' in "stage-*properties*," i.e. stage-requisites, actors'
equipments etc.

102. *advise you*, be careful; see G.

103. *Malvolio, Malvolio*; supposed to be said by Sir Topas.

104. *endeavour thyself*, strive. The reflexive use of verbs
which are now intransitive is a feature of Shakespearian English;
cf. v. 286.

105. *bibble-babble*, foolish talking; see G.

107. *Maintain no words.* A dialogue in two voices is supposed to go on between Sir Topas and the Clown (whose part here needs very clever acting). Sir Topas tells him not to talk to Malvolio, and then departs, his last word spoken aloud being *amen.*

109. *I will, Sir, I will;* "spoken (says Johnson) after a pause as if, in the mean-time, Sir Topas had whispered" to the Clown.

112. *shent,* reproved, i.e. by Sir Topas; see G.

131. A snatch from some old ballad; in singing it the Clown would use his tabor (III. i. 2). "Anon, anon, sir," was the regular phrase of innkeepers and tapsters; like our waiters' "Coming, sir."

134–141. The Vice, a personification of wickedness, and the Devil were traditional characters of the old 'Morality' plays, in which they represented the popular comic element. Each was marked by a traditional equipment. The Vice, in a long coat, a vizor and a cap with ass's ears, bore a *dagger of lath* (i.e. *soft* wood); the Devil, often dressed as a bear, had long talons and carried a club. The chief fun of the scenes in which they appeared was that the Vice belaboured the Devil with the dagger of lath and tried to cut his talons, i.e. *pare his nails.* Cf. *Henry V,* IV. 4. 75–77, "this roaring devil i' the old play...everyone may *pare his nails with a wooden dagger.*" In the end the Devil descended to the infernal regions with the Vice on his back. From the character of the Vice was developed the Fool or Clown of Shakespeare's plays. Stage-weapons are "dummies," to avoid wounds.

138. *ah, ha!*; the usual address of the Vice to the Devil in the Morality plays. These lines (138–141) represent what the Vice says to the Devil in the plays—not what the Clown says in his own character to Malvolio.

141. In Greene's *Friar Bacon* (1594), Scene xv, the Devil appears and is addressed by a character as "*goodman* friend." Possibly *good man* (see G.) was a traditional title for him.

The repetition of *devil* (cf. 138) does not seem to me awkward, the two stanzas being a piece of some doggerel ballad. But the "Globe" edition marks the line corrupt, and some editors change to *drivel.*

SCENE III.

2. *this pearl*; referring, no doubt, to an engagement ring.

6. *there he was,* i.e. he *had* been there, to bespeak entertainment (III. 3. 40); then he had gone about the town to look for Sebastian and been arrested, as we saw (III. 4. 360).

credit, report; literally 'a thing believed' (Lat. *creditum*).

12. *instance,* precedent, example. *discourse,* reason; see G.

15. *trust*, conviction.

18. Note that *take* (='undertake') applies to *affairs*, and *give back* (='settle') to *dispatch*.

21. *deceivable*, deceptive. In Elizabethan E. the termination *-able*, now commonly passive, was often active =*-ful*. We still have "changeable," ='full of change,' "peaceable," and others.

24. *chantry*, the small private chapel belonging to Olivia's house. In Italy, more than in England, large houses usually have a chapel.

26. In the light of v. 159 ("a contract") and 146–148 ("husband") this passage is now interpreted as a reference to, *not* the mere "betrothal" or "troth-plight" of an engaged couple, but an Elizabethan form of *civil* marriage, called the "contract of espousals." This "contract" was made before witnesses (cf. line 24), ratified with the gift of a ring, and "constituted a perfectly legal and valid marriage, though it required the religious solemnity ('celebration,' 30) to give the parties their legal status as regards property." It is believed that Shakespeare himself went through this form of "contract" with Anne Hathaway (afterwards through the religious rite), and that in this play and in *Measure for Measure*, IV. I. 72, he is alluding to his own case.

29. *Whiles*, until; cf. "*while* then" ='till then,' *Macbeth*, III. 1. 44.

30. *What time*, at which time, when.

34. *father*; the ordinary title of a priest; cf. v. 153.

35. *fairly note*, look favourably upon.

ACT V.

Scene I.

The lapse of time is shown by line 166.

1. *his letter*, i.e. Malvolio's letter to Olivia.

7, 8. Perhaps Shakespeare alludes to a contemporary anecdote. Manningham (see *Introduction*, p. x) relates in his *Diary* how "one Dr Bullein, the Queenes [i.e. Elizabeth's] kinsman, had a dog which he doted on soe much that the Queene understanding of it requested he would graunt her one desyre, and he should have what soever he would aske. Shee demaunded his dogge; he gave it. 'Nowe, Madame,' quoth he, 'you promised to give me my desyre.' 'I will,' quothe she. 'Then I pray you give me my dog againe.'"—*Notes and Queries*, 7. IV. 185. For another anecdote connected with Queen Elizabeth cf. *Richard II*, v. 5. 68.

10. *trappings*, belongings.

11. *I know thee*; the Clown had sung to Orsino (II. 4).

22. *abused*, deceived; cf. F. *abuser*.

23. *conclusions*, inferences: 'as it takes 2 negatives to make 1 affirmative, so it takes 2 people to make 1 kiss.' Throughout the play the Clown indulges in these sententious sayings, the point of which generally lies in the fact that they sound very wise or recondite, but in reality are very foolish or simple.

Some editors give another explanation suggested by the following passage in the play *Lust's Dominion* (earlier than *Twelfth Night*):

"*Queen.* Come, lets *kiss*.

Moor. Away, Away!

Queen. '*No, no*,' says '*aye*'; and twice '*away*' says '*stay*.'"

"*No, no*" makes 1 affirmative which ends in 1 kiss, and a second "*no, no*" makes 1 more affirmative which ends in 1 more kiss: hence the 4 negatives result in 2 kisses.

your four negatives. Shakespeare often uses *your* colloquially (cf. Latin *iste*), to indicate some person or thing known to everyone; e.g. in *Hamlet*, III. 2. 3, "you mouth it, as many of *your* players do," i.e. the players whom you and everybody know.

We have seen how Shakespeare himself ignores the fact that 4 negatives = 2 affirmatives by using 2 negatives = 1 strong affirmative.

32. *double-dealing*, duplicity; used, like *double-dealer* in 38, with a quibble. The Clown got a double present from Viola (III. 1).

35. *grace*, virtue. He quibbles on the sense, (1) 'pocket your virtue' (as we say), i.e. do not be too scrupulous, (2) 'put your gracious hand into your pocket,' i.e. take out your purse.

36. *obey it*; referring to either *grace* or *counsel* in 34.

37. *so much...to be*; understand *as*; cf. II. 4. 99.

39. *Primo, secundo, tertio*; probably a phrase used in some well-known game with dice; cf. "at this *throw*"='cast, venture,' 45.

41. *triplex*, triple time in music.

42. *Bennet*; short for *Benedick*. There was a well-known church of *St Bennet*, Paul's Wharf, destroyed in the Fire of London, 1666.

48. *lullaby to*, let it go to sleep—the metaphor suggested by "awake" in Orsino's speech.

57–60. *bawbling*, insignificant, trifling; see G. *For...draught*, in respect of its depth in the water. *unprizable*, valueless. *scathe-ful*, harmful—'full of *scathe*' (=damage). *bottom*, ship.

61. *envy...loss*; those who were mortified at sight of his

bravery and suffered loss through it. Abstract for concrete; see
I. 5. 307, note.

64-67. "Topical" allusions. A great English society, the
Levant Company (like the old East India Company) traded with
the Levant, i.e. Greece and the Greek islands, e.g. "Candy" =
Candia (Crete), and Asia Minor. Its headquarters in the East
was Aleppo, and the "Phœnix" and the "Tiger" were famous
London ships engaged in its trade. No doubt S. (and his
audience) had them in mind. Cf. too *Macbeth*, I. 3. 7, where
the witch says that "the master [captain] o' the Tiger" is gone
"to Aleppo" (i.e. to Tripoli in Syria, the port of Aleppo, an
inland city). In Antonio's exploits we get a glance at the pirates
with whom the Mediterranean was infested—the "water-thieves"
of *The Merchant of Venice*, I. 3. 22-25.

68. *brabble*, noisy brawl, quarrel.

69. *drew*, i.e. his sword. It is a pleasant touch that Viola at
once stands up for Antonio, using her influence on his behalf.

70. *put strange speech upon me*, talked to me in an odd manner.

71. *distraction*, madness; scan as four syllables; see I. I. 39,
note.

73. *their mercies*, the mercies of those who; cf. III. I. 69.

74. *so dear*, costing them so dear.

78. *on base and ground*, with good cause and reason.

82. *wreck*; see G.

85. *all his in dedication*, entirely devoted to his service.

86. *pure*, purely, entirely.

87. *into*, unto; a common use in Shakespeare.

89. *being apprehended*; understand *I*.

91. *face me out of his acquaintance*, pretend not to know me.

92. *twenty-years-removed*; such compound phrases are not
uncommon in Shakespeare; cf. *Richard II*, I. I. 180, "A jewel
in a *ten-times-barr'd-up* chest."

93. *While one*, in the time that it would take one to wink.

104. *but that*, save that which.

106. *promise*. Sebastian had promised to visit her and been
delayed—we see later the reason why.

109. A point which may be made amusing in actual representation of the play is Olivia's distraction between Orsino and
Cesario (Viola). She is longing to know why Cesario has not
"kept promise": yet courtesy requires that she should pay some
attention to the duke.

112. *fat*, distasteful; much the same as "fulsome."

121, 122. Shakespeare alludes to an episode in a very popular
Greek romance or novel, the *Aethiopica* of Heliodorus, a writer
of the second half of the fourth century A.D. The *Aethiopica*, so

called because the scene is laid partly in *Aethiopia*, was translated into many languages. There was an English version, published about 1568 and again in 1587, through which, doubtless, the
romance was known to Shakespeare and to many of his hearers,
so that they would understand the allusion. (See II. 5. 45, note.)

The "Egyptian thief" was *Thyamis*, a native of Memphis in
Egypt, captain of a band of robbers. He captured *Chariclea* (the
heroine) and her lover Theagenes, desired to marry her, and for
safety shut her up in a cave. Attacked by other robbers and
finding himself doomed to perish ("at point of death"), Thyamis
rushed to the cave to kill Chariclea, so that she might not fall
into the hands of his enemies; for "it was customary with those
barbarians, when they despaired of their own safety, first to
make away with those whom they held dear, and desired for
companions in the next life." In the darkness of the cave
Thyamis slew another woman, and Chariclea was saved.

123. *savours nobly*, has in it a relish of nobility; cf. 322.

125. *And that*, and because; *that*, a conjunction = '*for* that.'

126. *screws*, wrenches, forces.

128. *minion*, darling; see G.

129. *tender*; 'to treat kindly,' hence 'to hold dear' (as here).

131. *in his master's spite*, to the vexation of his master.

134. *raven...dove*; a proverbial contrast; cf. *Midsummer-
Night's Dream*, II. 2. 114, "Who will not change a raven for a
dove?"

136. *To do you rest*, to bring you peace of mind.

146–148. *husband*; note how emphasised; cf. *Measure for
Measure*, IV. 1. 72, "He is your husband on a pre-contract."
See IV. 3. 26, note.

149. *fear*, i.e. lest he (Cesario) should displease Orsino.

150. *strangle thy propriety*, disown what you really are, dis-
avow yourself. *Propriety* here means individuality—that which
is essentially a man's very own (Lat. *proprius*).

153. *fear'st*, i.e. to be.

156. *occasion*, necessity.

159. *A contract*, i.e. the "pre-contract" (as it is called in
Measure for Measure, IV. 1. 72) of marriage; see IV. 3. 26, note.

162. *interchangement*. It is still customary for an engaged
couple to give each other engagement rings.

168. *sow'd*, scattered, sprinkled. *grizzle*, a tinge of grey; cf.
Hamlet, I. 2. 240, "His beard was *grizzled*." Cf. F. *gris*, 'grey.'

case, skin; so called because it '*encases*' the body. "Every
man's *skinne* is the *case* of a sinner," said an Elizabethan divine,
Andrew Kingsmill (died 1569). In *All's Well That Ends Well*,
III. 6. 111, to '*case* the fox' means to strip off his skin.

169, 170. i.e. his own cunning will trip him up and ruin him.

174. *Hold little faith*, at least keep faith *a* little, i.e. do not perjure yourself by swearing falsely.

176. *presently*, immediately; see III. 4. 217.

179. *coxcomb*, head; see G.

181. *forty pound*; see II. 3. 20, note.

185. *incardinate*; Sir Andrew means *incarnate*. There is a similar mistake in *Henry V*, II. 3. 35, where the hostess confuses *incarnate* with *carnation* (the colour red).

187. *Od's*, a corruption of *God's*; we find it combined with other diminutives similar to *lifelings* ('a little life'). Cf. "od's heartlings," *Merry Wives*, III. 4. 59, "od's pittikins," *Cymbeline*, IV. 2. 293.

190–192. Viola refers to what took place in Act III, Scene 4; but since then Sir Andrew and Sir Toby have come across Sebastian—to their cost. *bespake you fair*, spoke courteously to you.

194. *set nothing by*, think nothing of.

198. *othergates*, in another manner; see G.

205. Cf. *The Tempest*, III. 2. 9, 10, "*Drink*, servant-monster: thy *eyes* are almost *set* in thy head." Probably the sense is 'closed'; cf. *King John*, v. 7. 51, "O cousin, thou art come to *set* mine *eye*" (spoken by the King just before he dies). But *set* might indicate the fixed, vacant stare of an intoxicated person.

206, 207. The 1st Folio has "*and* a passy measures *panyn*." The 2nd and other Folios have "*after* a passy measures *Pavin*." The reading in our text is made up from both versions.

Some editors take "pany*n*" as a misprint for "pany*m*" = 'a heathen,' the old form of *pagan*, and regard "passy measures" as Sir Toby's tipsy blunder for "passing measure." The general sense they interpret, 'He is a rogue and an egregious, extreme heathen.' This seems to me very far-fetched.

The reading in our text may be explained thus. There was an Italian dance called the *passamezzo*; it was a kind of *pavan* or *pavin*, also a dance. Like many foreign dances, the *passamezzo* was introduced into England, became pouplar in Elizabeth's reign, and is not infrequently mentioned in Elizabethan musical books. It was sometimes known as the '*passing measures* pavan'; and other corrupt, quasi-English forms of its Italian name, very similar to Sir Toby's *passy measures*, were in current use. See *pavin* in G.

Now the point of Sir Toby's remark must be sought for in the character of the music to which a passamezzo pavan was danced. Briefly, a tune of this type consisted of regular "strains," which in their turn usually contained *eight* bars each. In fact, "set at eight" would be a fair description of a tune for this pavan, and the description of the Surgeon's eyes started the idea in Sir Toby's thoughts. (Furness.)

212. *ass-head...coxcomb*; these reproaches seem to be addressed to Sir Andrew, of whom Sir Toby, in his intoxicated state, no longer conceals his real opinion. But he may refer to Sebastian.

Enter Sebastian. He does not see Viola till line 231.

217. *of my blood*, i.e. my own brother.

218. *wit and safety*; "a wise regard for safety" (Rolfe).

219. *a strange regard.* He mistakes her look of astonishment at the resemblance between him and Viola for a look of estrangement or reserve because he struck Sir Toby. Cf. *strange* in II. 5. 184. We may remember that the natural likeness between brother and sister was increased by the fact that she had imitated his dress (III. 4. 416–418).

224. *perspective*; a general term for *any* glass "cut in such a manner as to produce an optical deception, when looked through." Orsino meant that when he looked at Viola and Sebastian he saw, as if by an optical delusion, the same face twice over. *Perspectives* are often mentioned by Elizabethans and were of many kinds. Sometimes these glasses were called *prospectives*, e.g. in Greene's *Friar Bacon* (1594) VI. 110, where Roger Bacon's famous magical glass is referred to.

228. For the scansion 'Antón|io,' the *io* being slurred, cf. III. 3. 13, note. *Fear'st*; cf. *Merry Wives of Windsor*, IV. 4. 78, "*fear* not that," i.e. do not *doubt* it.

234, 235. *that deity*, that divine character or power. 'I cannot, like a god, be omnipresent—in all places at the same time.'

237. *Of charity*, in your kindness tell me; *of* = 'out of.' This old use of *charity* = 'benevolence' (Lat. *caritas*) survives in the phrase "Of your charity, pray." Cf. too "faith, hope, charity" (ἀγάπη).

240. *Such*, i.e. as you are.

241. *So...suited*, dressed as you are.

244. *dimension*, body (I. 5. 280). *grossly*, materially, or 'coarsely.'

246. *the rest goes even*, everything else corresponds, fits in.

253. *record*, recollection; scan probably *recórd. lively*, vivid.

254. *act*, career.

256. *lets*, hinders; see G.

259. *jump*, agree; see G.

261–263. See I. 2. 53–56.

262. *where*, at whose house. *weeds*, clothes; see G.

263. *preserv'd*; some editors alter to *preferr'd* = 'recommended.'

264. *occurrence of my fortune*, i.e. all my business, occupation.

266. *mistook*; on this form, instead of *mistaken*, see I. 5. 282, note.

267. *bias*, natural tendency; see G. Olivia's instinct as a woman drew her towards Viola, a woman.

271. *noble...blood*; Orsino knew Sebastian's father; cf. I. 2. 28.

272. *If this be so*; 'if there really are *two* separate people—and, so far as I can see, there is no mistake' (a parenthesis). *the glass*; a reference perhaps to the *perspective* of 224. Or the metaphor may be drawn from a weather-glass; it suits the notion of shipwreck in 273.

276. *over-swear*, swear again.

278. *orbed continent*, the sun. *orbed*, circular. Some interpret *continent* = 'receptacle,' from Lat. *continere*, 'to contain, hold.'

282. *upon some action*, in consequence of some lawsuit.

283. *durance*, prison.

285. *enlarge*, set at large, liberate.

287. *distract*, distracted, out of his mind; see G.

288. *extracting*, absorbing; "drawing other thoughts from my mind." The 2nd and later Folios have *exacting*.

289. *clearly*, completely; cf. *clean* = 'quite'—e.g. in *Othello*, I. 3. 366, "clean out of the way." *his*, i.e. his frenzy.

292. *hold at the stave's end*, a proverbial phrase = 'to keep, ward off.' Here *stave* = *staff*; cf. *staves*, the plural of *staff*.

295. *it skills not much*, it matters not; *skills*, see G.

299. *delivers*, i.e. utters the words of; quibbling on 'sets free.'

300. *By the Lord, madam*; probably the Clown shouts these words; then when Olivia, in surprise, reproves him, he says, 'you must not mind a loud voice (*vox*)—it is appropriate to a madman's letter.'

307. *perpend*, consider; an affected word which Shakespeare puts in the mouth only of Clowns and characters like the bombastic Pistol.

313. *cousin* = uncle; see G.

318. *my duty*, i.e. his respect to his mistress; he has been so wronged that he ventures to speak plainly to her.

324. *thought on*, having been considered; an absolute construction.

327. *at my proper cost*, at my expense. *proper*, own.

328, 329. *apt*, ready. *quits you*, releases you from service.

330. *mettle*, character, natural disposition.

334. Viola will be Olivia's "sister" doubly—through Sebastian, Olivia's husband, and through Orsino who henceforth regards Olivia as his "sweet sister" (393).

335. *Is this the madman?*; said in surprise. Orsino does not think that Malvolio looks mad.

337. *notorious*; cf. IV. 2. 94.

339. *you must not*, it is no use for you to.

340. *from it*, i.e. differently. Cf. II. 5. 102, "her very *phrases*."

341. *your seal*; cf. II. 5. 103, "her Lucrece."

344. *clear lights*, distinct marks.

347. *the lighter people*, my inferiors. *light*, 'of no importance.'

350, 351. i.e. "visited" officially as a lunatic. *geck*, dupe; see G.

354. *character*, hand-writing; Gk. χαρακτήρ, 'an engraved mark.'

356, 357. *she first told me*; see III. 4. 8–14. *cam'st*; understand *thou* from "*thou* wast mad."

358. *such which*, such *as. presuppos'd upon*, previously suggested to.

360. *practice*, trick. *most shrewdly*, in a very cruel way.

369. *upon*; literally 'following upon,' hence 'in consequence of.'

370, 371. *conceived against*; they had experienced (or 'seemed to find') *in* Malvolio certain faults which set them *against* him. To screen Maria from the annoyance of Olivia, who had hinted at punishment (361–363), Fabian puts the blame on Sir Toby.

importance, importunity; cf. *King John*, II. 7, "at our importance is he come," i.e. at our urgent request. So *important* = 'importunate,' *Much Ado*, II. 1. 74 ("if the prince be too important, tell him").

372. *he hath married her*; see IV. 2. 75, note.

374. *pluck on*, excite.

375. *the injuries*. No doubt, Malvolio used his authority in the house oppressively; Fabian had special cause of resentment (II. 5. 9, 10). And Maria, we may be sure, had always been jealous of Malvolio's influence with Olivia.

377. *poor fool!*; often in Shakespeare a term of pity. Olivia is sorry for Malvolio and would not say anything discourteous to him. *baffled*, treated ignominiously; see G.

378–385. Here the Clown takes his full revenge, reminding Malvolio of the 3 scenes in which he had cut the most ridiculous figure, viz. II. 5, III. 4 and IV. 2. The sentence "By the Lord, fool," is not a quotation but a summary, as it were, of Malvolio's remarks in the "dark room." In "Madam, why laugh you?" Malvolio hears his own words turned against himself; see I. 5. 89–94.

380. *thrown*; the Clown's slip for *thrust*; he quotes from memory.

interlude, play, i.e. their sport against Malvolio; see G.

385. *the whirligig*, the revolving course; a whirligig is "any toy or trivial object to which a rapid whirling motion is imparted," especially a top. Here the metaphor is rather that of a wheel going round; cf. the notion of "Fortune's wheel," where the wheel symbolises the vicissitudes (Lat. *vicissim*, 'by turn') of life. See II. 4. 117, note.

391. *golden*, auspicious. *convents*, suits, is *convenient*.

396, 397. *habits*, dress (Lat. *habitus*); cf. 'riding-*habit*.' *fancy*, love.

Exeunt all, except Clown. Describing the ordinary performance of an Elizabethan drama, Dowden notes how at the end of the play the Clown used to "put the audience into good humour before they separated with...a farcical song accompanied by dancing and the music of his pipe or *tabor*." The song and dance were called the "jig"; generally a second performer took part in it.

"The jesters were, without doubt, the bright particular stars of the companies to which they belonged, the most popular of the actors, and the best remunerated" (Raleigh). The most famous of them in Shakespeare's time was Will Kemp.

Song. This, like some of the other Songs in the play, seems to be an old popular ballad, perhaps adapted by Shakespeare. The 'burden' or refrain, i.e. the two lines repeated in each stanza, occurs in a stanza of a similar ballad sung by the Fool in *Lear*, III. 2. 74–77.

398. *When that*; cf. *Julius Cæsar*, III. 2. 96, "When that the poor have cried, Caesar hath wept." For *that* added to conjunctions, see I. 2. 48, note. *and a tiny*; this redundant *and* is common in ballads.

399. *Hey* and *ho* occur frequently in ballad-refrains. Cf. *As You Like It*, v. 3. 18, "With a *hey*, and a *ho*, and a *hey* nonino."

400. 'My foolish deeds were thought little of when I was a boy: not so when I came to manhood (402); *then* men's doors were shut against me (404).' *toy*, trifle; see G.

ADDENDA TO THE NOTES

II. 3. 81. *Peg-a-Ramsey*, 'Margaret of Ramsey.' Ramsey in Huntingdonshire was formerly a town of some importance, noted for its great Abbey. *Peg* (whence the diminutive *Peggy*) is a variant of *Meg* (= *Mag*), short for *Margaret*.

II. 3. 124. *Cakes and ale.* "It was the custom on holidays and saints' days to make cakes in honour of the day. The Puritans called this superstition"; and Malvolio was "a kind of Puritan" (151).

II. 3. 161. *cons state*. Cf. "arguments of *state*" in Maria's letter (II. 5) and Malvolio's comment, "I will read *politic* authors," i.e. political writers. Surely, she must refer here not to his study of etiquette and deportment, but to his pompous style and "humour of state" (II. 5. 58). The satire is at the vanity which leads a "steward" to imagine himself little less than the Prime Minister of Illyria!

without book; having learnt it all by heart like an actor; for the stage-metaphor see I. 5. 186, note, and *Romeo*, I. 4. 6, 7.

II. 4. 115. *thought*, sadness, melancholy brooding; cf. the kindred meaning 'anxiety,' as in "take no thought for your life"="be not anxious" (Revised Version), *Matt.* v. 25.

II. 5. 167. *cross-gartered*, i.e. with garters worn below the knee, crossed at the back of the leg and fastened in a bow above the knee.

III. 1. 25. *Words are very rascals* etc., i.e. words have become very dangerous things to deal with since such restrictions ("bonds") have been put on the stage. Some interpret 'words are disgraced by being used in contracts' ("bonds") i.e. for legal and financial trickeries.

III. 1. 132. *a cyprus, not a bosom*. Olivia quibbles on *bosom*= 'the bosom of a dress,' which would not be transparent like "cyprus." Probably this is the point in *Midsummer-Night's Dream*, II. 2. 104, 105.

III. 4. 258. *on carpet consideration*. Some think that *consideration* implies that Sir Andrew had purchased his knighthood. The word does not convey this idea of 'monetary consideration' elsewhere in Shakespeare.

IV. 1. 14, 15. *lubber...cockney*. To an Elizabethan the words would be absolutely antithetic, and in this antithesis lies the verbal wit. Changes like *lubberly word* (="vent") are valueless. The original text, with Johnson's interpretation ("affectation and foppery will overspread the world") holds the field. The sense turns on the history of *cockney*.

V.206,207. Dr Naylor's explanation ("The doctor's eyes were 'set at eight,' and so is a Pavan 'set at eight'") is convincing. The old one was that Sir Toby, who likes brisk dances (I. 3. 137, 138), uses the name of the "pavan," a grave stately dance, contemptuously, to imply that the Surgeon is 'a grave solemn coxcomb' and slow in coming.

GLOSSARY

A.S. = Anglo-Saxon, i.e. English down to about the Conquest.

Middle E. = Middle English, i.e. English from about the Conquest to about 1500.

Elizabethan E. = the English of Shakespeare and his contemporaries (down to about 1650).

O.F. = Old French, i.e. till about 1600. F. = modern French.

Germ. = modern German. Gk = Greek.

Ital. = modern Italian. Lat. = Latin.

Note: In using the Glossary the student should pay very careful attention to the context in which each word occurs.

abuse; in IV. 2. 51, 95 = 'to use ill, maltreat'; in V. 22 = 'to deceive,' like F. *abuser*. For the latter, cf. *The Tempest*, V. 112, "some enchanted trifle to abuse me."

access, I. 4. 16. Shakespeare commonly accents *accéss*. Many words now accented on the first syllable were in Elizabethan English accented on the second syllable, i.e. they retained the French accent, which (roughly speaking) was that of the original Latin words. By "accent" one means, of course, the stress laid by the voice on any syllable in pronouncing it. Thus we say *prócess*; but Milton wrote "By policy and long *procéss* of time" (*Paradise Lost*, II. 297); cf. French *procès*, Lat. *procéssus*. So Shakespeare scans *aspéct*, *commérce*, *edíct*, when it suits him.

accost, I. 3. 52; not used by Shakespeare in any other play. Both the sense and the form in which it occurs here (I. 3. 52) were uncommon. The usual spelling then was *accoast* (Lat. *ad* + *costa*, 'a rib,' whence *coast*).

admire, III. 4. 165; in the literal sense of Lat. *admirari*, 'to wonder'; cf. Milton, *Paradise Lost*, II. 677, 678:

"The undaunted Fiend what this might be admired,
    Admired, not feared."

So *admirable* = 'to be wondered at,' *Midsummer-Night's Dream*, V. 27, "strange and admirable."

advise, IV. 2. 102; often reflexive in Elizabethan E. = 'consider,' like F. *s'aviser*. Cf. 1 *Chronicles* xxi. 12, "advise thyself what word I shall bring" (Revised Version "consider").

affectioned, II. 3. 160, 'affected,' literally 'full of *affection*'

(=affectation); cf. the Quarto's reading (1604) in *Hamlet*, II. 2. 464, "no matter in the phrase that might indict the author of *affection*," where the Folio (1623) substitutes *affectation*. The same discrepancy between the 1st Folio and the 2nd (1632) occurs in *Love's Labour's Lost*, V. 2. 407. The inference is that this use of *affection* had become rather old-fashioned.

allow, I. 2. 59, 'approve'; cf. *2 Henry IV*, IV. 2. 54, "I like them all, and do allow them well." So *Romans* vii. 15, "that which I do I allow not." Lat. *allaudare*, 'to praise.'

an. Note that—(1) *an* is a weakened form of *and* (*d* often drops off from the end of a word: cf. *lawn*=*laund*); (2) *and*='if' was a regular use; (3) till about 1600 this full form *and*, not the shortened form *an*, was commonly printed. Cf. Bacon, *Essays* (23), "They will set an house on fire, *and* it were but to roast their egges"; *Matthew* xxiv. 48, "But *and if* that evil servant shall say." The Quartos and 1st Folio (1623) of Shakespeare often have *and* where modern texts print *an*.

How *and* or *an* came to mean 'if' is much disputed.

attend, III. 4. 243, 'wait for'=F. *attendre*. Cf. *Merry Wives of Windsor*, I. 1. 279, "the dinner attends you"; *Hamlet*, V. 2. 205, "attend him in the hall."

ay me, V. 142, 'alas.' Cf. Milton, *Lycidas*, 56, "Ay me! I fondly dream." From O.F. *aymi*, 'alas for me!'; cf. Gk. οἴμοι.

baffle. Originally (1) 'to inflict public disgrace upon,' especially upon a perjured or cowardly knight; cf. *Faerie Queene*, VI. 7. 27. Hence (2) 'to treat with contempt,' as in II. 5. 175. Also (3) 'to fool, gull,' as probably in V. 377. Cf. Milton's prose work, *The Likeliest Means* (1659), "men will not be gulled and baffled."

barricado, IV. 2. 41; Spanish *barricada*, from *barrica*, 'a barrel.' Properly *barricado*='a rampart hastily formed out of barrels, stones etc.'; hence=any 'barrier or obstruction.' Also used as a verb='to fortify'; cf. *Paradise Lost*, VIII. 241, "The dismal gates...barricadoed strong."

bawbling, V. 57, 'insignificant, paltry'; literally 'worth or like a bauble,' i.e. a useless toy. Cf. *Troilus and Cressida*, I. 3. 35, "shallow *bauble* boats." A vessel is regarded as the plaything of the waves.

bawcock, III. 4. 125. A colloquial, rather contemptuous, term of endearment='fine fellow, good fellow,' much the same as *chuck*. Cf. *Henry V*, III. 2. 26, "Good *bawcock*, bate thy rage; use lenity, sweet *chuck*." F. *beau coq*.

be, II. 2. 33, II. 3. 82. The root *be* was conjugated in the present tense, singular and plural, up till about the middle of the 17th century. The singular, indeed, was almost limited in Elizabethan E. to the phrase, "if thou beest," common in Shake-speare; cf. *Tempest*, v. 134, "If thou beest Prospero." For the plural, cf. *Genesis* xlii. 32, "we be twelve brethren."

beshrew. Generally combined with *me* or *my heart*, either as a mild imprecation 'woe to' (cf. IV. 1. 62), or for emphasis 'indeed' (cf. II. 3. 85). The original notion was 'to invoke some-thing *shrewd*, i.e. bad, on a person'; cf. the old use of *shrewd* = 'bad,' as in "foul shrewd news," i.e. bad news, *King John*, v. 5. 14. So *shrewdly* in v. 360 implies 'badly,' 'in a shameful way.'

bias, v. 267, 'natural tendency'; cf. *Lear*, I. 2. 120, "bias of nature." F. *biais*, 'a slope, slant.' The metaphorical use of *bias* = 'inclination, tendency' is taken from the game of bowls (a favourite Elizabethan pastime), the *bias* being the leaden weight inserted in the side of the bowl to make it run in a slanting line and incline a certain way. Cf. *Richard II*, III. 4. 5, "my fortune *runs against the bias*."

bibble-babble, IV. 2. 105, 'idle talk'; Fluellen, the Welsh-man, mispronounces it *pibble pabble* in *Henry V*, IV. 1. 71. Cf. *fiddle-faddle, tittle-tattle, pit-pat*. In each case the *second* half of the compound (e.g. *babble*) is reduplicated for emphasis, the vowel *a* weakening to *i*.

bird-bolt, I. 5. 100; a short arrow, with a broad flat end, discharged from a cross-bow; used to shoot small birds with, as it would just stun the bird without spoiling the plumage or flesh.

blab, I. 2. 63, 'to reveal something which should be kept secret.' Cf. Coverdale (1535), *Proverbs* xvi. 29, "He yᵗ [that] is a blabbe of his tonge, maketh devysion amonge prynces." Now a colloquial word.

blazon, I. 5. 312. Originally (1) 'A shield used in war.' Then (2) 'a shield in heraldry,' and so 'armorial bearings, a *coat* of arms'—its sense here. Cf. *Merry Wives*, v. 5. 67, 68, "each... *coat* and several *crest* with loyal *blazon*." Later (3) 'a banner bearing arms'; cf. Macaulay, *Armada* 20, "Slow upon the labouring wind the royal blazon swells."

breast, II. 3. 20, 'voice'; cf. Ben Jonson, *The Gipsies Meta-morphosed* (1621), "An excellent *song*, and a sweet *songster!* a fine *breast!*"

buttery-bar, I. 3. 74. *Buttery*, from O.F. *boterie*, 'bottles,' meant a store-room (1) for liquor, (2) for any provisions. The word is still in general use at Oxford and Cambridge Colleges. The opening—a kind of half door—at which the provisions were served out from the store-room was called the *buttery-hatch*, and the ledge or bar on the top of it, whereon to place things, was the *buttery-bar*. F. *bouteille* and *bottle*, *butler* (originally *boteler*) are cognate with *buttery*, which in etymology has nothing to do with *butter*.

canary, I. 3. 85; a favourite Elizabethan wine imported from the *Canary* Isles. Many wines are called after the place where they are made—e.g. *port* from *Oporto* and *sherry* from *Xeres*. See *sack*.

canton, I. 5. 289, 'song'; cf. *Zepheria* (1594), 11, "How many Cantons then sent I to thee." Only here in Shakespeare; the form is perhaps a confusion between *canto* and *canzon* (also rare) = Ital. *canzone*, 'song, ballad'; cf. Lodge, *Euphues Golden Legacie* (1590), "My canzon was written in no such humor."

Cataian, or **Cathaian**, II. 3. 80; literally 'a native of *Cathay*' (China); also a term of reproach = 'thief, rogue,' from the thieving propensity of the Chinese attributed to them in many old books of travels (Nares). Cf. *Merry Wives*, II. 1. 148, "I will not believe such a Cataian." Then *Cathay* was the ordinary name of China, being a corruption of *Kitai*, the name by which China is still known in Russia and Asia.

catch, II. 3. 18, 60; a short musical composition for three or more voices unaccompanied, "which sing the same melody, the second singer beginning the first line as the first goes on to the second line, and so with each successive singer"; called a *catch* because each singer has to *catch* or take up his part in time. The peculiarity of many catches is that the words and lines are so arranged as to produce comical effects. This was the case with the catch sung by Sir Andrew and the others. The modern term for such pieces, essentially English, is a "round."

caterwauling, II. 3. 76. *Cater* is from *cat*, the *er* being a connecting sound between the parts of the compound; *waul* is an imitative word.

Such words illustrate the principle of *onomatopœia*, i.e. the formation of a word which in its *sound* imitates or suggests the thing or action signified. Thus the word *peewit* is an imitation of the bird's cry. Many words are formed in this way; cf. *lullaby*, *peevish*, *daw* (III. 4. 38).

champaign, II. 5. 173, or **champain**, 'flat open country.' Cf. *Lear*, I. 1. 65, "With shadowy forests and with champaigns rich'd." F. *campagne*, Ital. *campagna*, from Lat. *campus*, 'a plain.'

cheveril, III. 1. 13, 'kid leather'; O.F. *chevrel* (modern F. *chevreau*), 'a kid.' Such soft leather naturally symbolises something flexible, easily stretched or turned. Cf. *Henry VIII*, II. 3. 32, 33, "your *soft cheveril conscience*...if you might please to *stretch* it."

clear-stories, IV. 2. 41. The *clear-* (commonly spelt *clere-*)

story windows of churches are those small upper windows above the arches of the nave (i.e. above the triforium, if there is one). Though chiefly used of churches, *clere-story* was also applied to similar windows in large halls such as the college-halls at Oxford and Cambridge. Here the application of so grand a word to Malvolio's "dark room" is intentional humour. From *clear*, 'lighted' + *story*, 'floor of a building.'

cloistress, I. I. 28, 'nun,' i.e. one who lives in a *cloister* = Late Lat. *claustrum* or *clostrum* = 'a monastery,' from *claudere*, 'to shut.'

cockney, IV. I. 15. Its meanings may be traced thus: (1) 'a spoilt child, favourite, minion'—the commonest sense from about 1400 to about 1600; cf. Nash, *Pierce Penilesse*, 18, "A young heyre [i.e. *heir*], or cockney, that is his mothers darling." Hence (2) 'an effeminate, affected person'—as here (IV. I. 15); especially an affected, squeamish woman—as in *Lear*, II. 4. 123. Then (3) 'a native of a town,' townsmen being often effeminate compared with country folk. Hence (4) 'a native of London' as being *the* town of England. Its etymology has nothing to do with the fabulous 'land of *Cocaigne*.'

comfortable, I. 5. 239, 'comforting, full of comfort'; cf. *Richard II*, II. 2. 76, "speak comfortable words." Cf. also *Isaiah* xl. 2, "Speak ye comfortably to Jerusalem."

competitor, IV. 2. 12, 'associate, partner'; cf. *Antony and Cleopatra*, II. 7. 76, "These three world-*sharers*, these *competitors*." Now *competitor* = 'rival.' Lat. *cum*, 'with' + *petere*, 'to seek.'

complexion, II. 4. 27; 5. 30; then a word of wider scope, often equivalent to 'external appearance in general.' Originally *complexion* was an old physiological term for 'the combination of the four "humours" of the body in a certain proportion'; hence 'the nature, temperament' arising from this combination, as in *Hamlet*, I. 4. 27, *The Merchant of Venice*, III. 1. 32. Lat. *complexio* used in Late Lat. = 'bodily constitution, habit,' from *complectere*, 'to embrace, combine.'

coranto, I. 3. 137, 'a quick, lively dance'; cf. *Henry V*, III. 5. 33, "*swift* corantos." From Ital. *coranta*; cf. the French form *courante*, 'a *running* dance,' from *courir*, Lat. *currere*. It seems to have been introduced from France into Italy, and thence into England.

county, I. 5. 320, 'count'; cf. *Romeo*, III. 5. 219, "I think it best you married with the *county*," i.e. Count Paris. The *y* (*count-y*) represents the *e* of O.F. *conte*, modern F. *comté* (Lat. *comes*); cf. another Elizabethan form *countee*. Cf. Scott's "County Guy" (*Quentin Durward*).

cousin; used by Shakespeare of any degree of kinship (except the first, as father, son); e.g. = 'niece' (I. 3. 5); = 'uncle' (I. 5. 131, V. 313). Sometimes in Shakespeare *cousin* is merely a friendly title " given by princes to other princes and distinguished noblemen."

coxcomb, V. 179, 193; properly (1) 'a fool's cap,' so called because like a cock's comb in shape and colour; then (2) a jocular term for the head. Cf. *Henry V*, V. 1. 57, "the skin [of the leek] is good for your *broken coxcomb*" (Fluellen has just struck Pistol on the head).

coystril, I. 3. 43, 'a mean paltry fellow'; from F. *coustillier*, 'a groom,' literally 'one who carries a dagger.' F. *coustille* = 'dagger,' from Lat. *cultellus*, 'a little knife' (*culter*). The *coustillier* bore his master's weapons (like a golf-caddy) and attended him in battle.

cozier, II. 3. 97, 'cobbler'; F. *couseur*, 'one who sews,' from *coudre*, 'to sew' (cf. the present participle *cousant*).

crowner, I. 5. 142, a colloquial form of *coroner*; cf. *Hamlet*, V. 1. 24, "crowner's quest [inquest] law" (spoken by one of the grave-diggers). Literally 'a *crown*-officer,' Lat. *coronator*.

curst, III. 2. 46 = *cursed*, the p. p. of *curse*; through colloquial use *curst* lost something of its original force and in Shakespeare commonly means 'shrewish' (especially used so of women), 'sharp-tongued,' 'ill-tempered.' In *The Taming of the Shrew* the heroine is called "Katharine the curst" (I. 2. 128), "Kate the curst" (II. 187).

cypress, or **cyprus**, III. 1. 132, a kind of crape or gauze material, usually black; cf. *The Winter's Tale*, IV. 4. 221, "Cypress *black* as e'er was crow," and Milton, *Il Penseroso*, 35, "*sable* stole of cypress lawn." Probably so called from the island of *Cyprus* (whence various fabrics were introduced into England through the Crusades); cf. *cambric* from *Cambray* in Flanders, *calico* from *Calicut*, and see *fustian*, p. 144. The peculiarity of cypress, which gives point to Olivia's remark, is its transparency.

damask, II. 4. 115, 'red, rosy.' The Syrian city of *Damascus* was famous for its red roses, and a favourite species called the "Damask rose" was (and is) much cultivated in England. Cf. Bacon, *Natural History*, "*Damaske-Roses*...have not been known in England above a hundred years, and now [1627] are so common." In Shakespeare *damask* implies either red or red and white mixed. Here 'red' seems likelier; cf. *Coriolanus*, II. 1. 232, "the war of white and *damask* in their...*cheeks*" (an allusion perhaps to the Wars of the Roses).

discourse, IV. 3. 12, 'reasoning'; cf. "discourse of reason" =

'power of reasoning' in *Troilus and Cressida*, II. 2. 116, and *Hamlet*, I. 2. 150. Then a common use of the word. Milton (*Paradise Lost*, v. 488, 489) makes the archangel Raphael say to Adam that there are two kinds of Reason, "*discursive*, or intuitive," and that men have the lower kind, viz. *discourse*, and Angels the higher, viz. *intuition*.

distract, v. 287, i.e. distract*ed* = 'mad'; Lat. *distractus*, the past participle of *distrahere*.

A noticeable point in Elizabethan English is the tendency to make the past participles of verbs of Latin origin conform with the Latin forms. This is the case especially with verbs of which the Latin originals belong to the 1st and 3rd conjugations. Thus Shakespeare and Milton have many participles like 'create' (*creatus*), 'consecrate' (*consecratus*), 'incorporate,' 'dedicate,' where the termination -*ate*, in modern English -*ated*, = Lat. -*atus*, the passive participial termination of the 1st conjugation; cf. **reverberate**, I. 5. 291.

So with the Latin 3rd conjugation; Latinised participles such as 'deject' (*dejectus*), 'distract,' 'attent' (*attentus*), 'suspect,' 'addict' (*addictus*), 'pollute' (*pollutus*), with many others, are to be found in Shakespeare or Milton. Further, participles not from the Latin are abbreviated by analogy; e.g. Milton (*Paradise Lost*, I. 193) has 'uplift' = 'uplift*ed*,' though *lift* is of Scandinavian origin.

ducat, I. 3. 22, a coin formerly worth in England about 6*s*. 8*d*. O.F. *ducat* from Italian *ducato*, so called because the *ducat* was first coined in the *duchy* (Lat. *ducatus*) of Apulia and bore the words "sit tibi, Christe, datus, quem tu regis, iste *ducatus*."

duello, III. 4. 337, 'the prescribed rules of duelling'; cf. *Love's Labour's Lost*, I. 2. 185, "the duello he regards not." In Ben Jonson's *Cynthia's Revels*, I. 1 a character returned from Italy (see p. 136) speaks of himself as the "first that ever enrich'd his country with the true laws of the duello." A famous Italian book (by Vincentio Saviolo) dealing with the whole etiquette of duelling had been translated into English in 1595, and is referred to in *As You Like It*, v. 4. 94. Ital. *duello*, literally 'a combat between two' (Lat. *duo*).

element. It was an old belief (to which Sir Toby alludes, II. 3. 10) that all existing things consist of *four elements* or constituent parts, viz. fire, water, earth and air; and that in the human body these *elements* appear as four 'humours'—fire = choler, water = phlegm, earth = melancholy, air = blood. Cf. *Henry V*, III. 7. 22, 23, "he is pure *air* and *fire*; and the dull *elements* of *earth* and *water* never appear in him." Then the word came to be specially used of one *element*, viz. the air and sky; cf. I. I. 26, and *Julius Cæsar*, I. 3. 128, "the complexion of the element," i.e. the appearance of the sky. By metaphor *element* signified 'natural sphere, proper habitation,' as in 'out of one's element'; cf. III. I. 65, III. 4. 137.

extent, IV. I. 57; "in law, a writ of execution, whereby goods are seized for the king. It is therefore taken here for *violence* in general" (Johnson). Cf. *As You Like It*, III. I. 17, "Make an extent upon his house and lands." The metaphorical use of a legal term is quite in Shakespeare's style. Schmidt takes *extent* = 'behaviour, conduct'; but it is doubtful whether the word ever bore that meaning.

fadge, II. 2. 34, 'to turn out well, succeed'; cf. *Love's Labour's Lost*, V. I. 154, "We will have, if this fadge not, an antique," i.e. if this fails. So in Lyly's *Mother Bombie* (1594), I. I, "I'll have thy advice, and if it fadge, thou shalt eat."

fall, I. I. 4, 'cadence'; cf. Pope, *St Cecilia's Day*,

"Till, by degrees, remote and small,
        The strains decay,
        And melt away,
        In a dying, dying fall."

Note the same metaphor in *cadence* (Lat. *cadere*, 'to fall').

fancy...fantastical, I. I. 14, 15. Here etymology has a literary value. *Fancy* is short for *fantasy*, Gk φαντασία, 'a making visible,' hence 'imagination.' So *fancy* = 'love' connotes love on its imaginative side; it means rather that the imagination has been captivated than that the heart has been won—as with Orsino.

favour, II. 4. 24, III. 4. 363, 'face, countenance.' Cf. *Richard II*, IV. 168, "I well remember the favours of these men." So *well-favoured* (I. 5. 169) = 'of good looks, handsome'; cf. *Genesis* xxix. 17, "Rachel was beautiful and well favoured." First *favour* meant (1) 'kindness,' then (2) 'expression of kindness in the face,' then (3) the face itself.

fraught, V. 64, 'cargo'; cf. *Titus Andronicus*, I. 71, "as the bark, that hath discharged her fraught." So *fraughtage* = 'cargo,' *Comedy of Errors*, IV. I. 87. Akin perhaps to *freight*.

fustian, II. 5. 119. Properly 'coarse cotton stuff,' so called from Arabic *fustát*, a name of Cairo in Egypt whence the stuff was first imported into England (see p. 142). By metaphor *fustian* means 'something high sounding and nonsensical'; Pistol was "a fustian rascal," *2 Henry IV*, II. 4. 203. Cf. *bombast*, literally = 'cotton-wadding to stuff out garments,' then metaphorically 'puffed up, affected language.'

galliard, I. 3. 127, 'a lively dance,' of Spanish origin; cf. *Henry V*, I. 2. 252, "a nimble galliard." Often mentioned together with *coranto* (see p. 141); cf. Selden's *Table-Talk*, 1654,

"At a solemn dancing, first you had the grave measures [i.e. slow dances], then the *corantoes*, and the *galliards*," Reynolds' ed. p. 93. Spanish *gallarda*.

geck, v. 351, 'dupe,' i.e. one who has been made a fool of. Cf. *Cymbeline*, v. 4. 67, 68, "the geck and scorn O' the other's villany." A word of Dutch origin; cf. Germ. *geck*, 'a fool, fop.'

gin, II. 5. 92, 'a snare, trap'; cf. *Isaiah* viii. 14, "he shall be... for a gin and for a snare." Short for *engin* (Lat. *ingenium*) used in Middle E. ='a contrivance, device,' i.e. something *ingeniously* made.

goodman, IV. 2. 141; properly 'master of the house,' *pater-familias*—cf. *Matthew* xx. 11, "they murmured against the good-man of the house"; just as *goodwife* (whence *goody*) ='mistress of the house.' But *goodman* and *goodwife* were used in addressing people of humble rank, such as the grave-digger in *Hamlet*, v. 1. 14, and a maid-servant in *Merry Wives of Windsor*, II. 2. 36.

grain, I. 5. 255. O.F. *graine* = Low Lat. *granum* which, like the classical Lat. *coccum*, was used of the scarlet dye made from the *cochineal* insect found on the scarlet oak. Cf. North's *Plutarch* (1579), "this sail...was *red, dyed in grain*, and of the colour of *scarlet*" (*Life of Theseus*). *Grain* was a strong, lasting dye—in fact, a 'fast' colour, i.e. one that would not fade or *wash out*. Cf. *Comedy of Errors*, III. 2. 107–109, "That's a fault that *water* will mend"..."No, sir, '*tis in grain*; Noah's flood could not do it," i.e. wash it off. Similarly the "red" (line 256) of Olivia's complexion was lasting. (*Grain* ='fibre of wood, tex-ture' is the same word; but the reference here is to the rosy hue, not to the texture, of Olivia's cheek. Cf. Milton, *Comus*, 750, "*cheeks* of sorry *grain*," i.e. hue, colour.)

grize, III. 1. 135; a rare obsolete form of *grece*, 'a flight of stairs or steps, a staircase'; from *gree*, 'a step.' The variant forms of this old word *grece* were very numerous—e.g. *greece, greese, grise*. It was quite common in older English, but here and in *Othello*, I. 3. 237 Shakespeare practically explains it. It has been remarked as a good illustration of "popular etymology" (i.e. in-correct notions as to the origin and meaning of words) that *Grecian* in the name of a flight of steps at Lincoln, popularly called "the *Grecian* stairs," is a corruption of some plural form of this old word *grece*. The original name would be simply 'the *greesen*' (or *grisen*) ='the steps'; then, as the word fell out of use, people would insert 'steps,' and soon 'the *greesen* steps' would be corrupted. Cf. Wyclif, *Exodus* xx. 26, "thou schalt not stye [ascend] by *grees* to myn auter" = "Neither shalt thou go up *by steps* unto mine altar" (Authorised Version). O.F. *gre*, Lat. *gradus*; cf. 'de-*gree*.'

haggard, III. 1. 71, 'a wild, untrained hawk'; cf. *The Taming* *of the Shrew*, IV. 1. 196, "Another way I have to man [i.e. tame] my haggard." F. *hagard*, 'wild'; especially a wild falcon.

his. The idiom seen in "'gainst the *count his* galleys" was common; cf. *Troilus and Cressida*, IV. 5. 177, "by *Mars his* gauntlet, thanks!" It arose from the old notion that the *'s* which marks the possessive case was a contraction of *his*—as though "the count *his*" were the true form, and "the count*'s*" a shortened form. Shakespeare commonly uses this wrong kind of genitive with proper names ending in *s*, such as *Mars*; no doubt, to avoid the awkward sound *Mars'* or *Mars's*. (For a good note on the point see A. S. West's *English Grammar*, p. 97, Pitt Press Series.)

hob, nob, or **hab, nab,** III. 4. 262; "compounded of *hab* and *nab*, to have or not to have. *Hab* is from A.S. *hæbban*, to have; *nab* is from A.S. *næbban*, put for *ne hæbban*, not to have" (Skeat). Elizabethan writers apply the phrase to reckless, headlong deeds which "make or mar"; cf. the explanation of it in Cotgrave (1611), "hit or miss."

hull, I. 5. 217; properly 'to drift to and fro on the water, like the *hull* of a ship without sails or rudder'; hence 'to float.' Cf. Gervase Markham's *Sir Richard Grenvile*, "Then casts he anchor hulling on the main." Milton speaks of the Ark "hulling" on the Flood, *Paradise Lost*, XI. 840.

interlude, V. 380, 'sport, comedy'; properly 'a play performed in the intervals of a festivity'—from Lat. *inter*, 'between' + *ludere*, 'to play.' The "most lamentable *comedy*" of Pyramus and Thisbe in *Midsummer-Night's Dream* is called an *interlude* (I. 2. 6, v. 156).

jet, II. 5. 36, 'to strut, stalk pompously'; cf. *Cymbeline*, III. 3. 5, "gates...that giants may jet through." O.F. *jetter*, 'to throw,' from Lat. *jactare*; the notion in *jet* is 'to fling oneself about in walking.' Cf. *swagger*, literally = 'to *sway* from side to side.'

jump, V. 259, 'agree, tally'; cf. *The Taming of the Shrew*, I. 1. 195, "Both our inventions meet and jump in one." So "jump *with*" = 'agree with'; cf. 1 *Henry IV*, I. 2. 78, "it jumps with my humour." Hence the adverb *jump* = 'exactly, just'; cf. *Othello*, II. 3. 392, "And bring him jump when he may Cassio find."

kickshaws, I. 3. 122, 'trifle'; from F. *quelque chose*, 'something.' Commonly applied to cookery = 'delicacy,' 'fanciful dish'; cf. 2 *Henry IV*, V. 1. 29, "a joint of mutton, and any pretty kickshaws."

leasing, I. 5. 105, 'falsehood'; cf. *Psalm* v. 6, "Thou shalt destroy them that speak leasing." A.S. *leásung*, 'falsehood,' from *leás*, 'false,' akin to *loose*; the notion in *leasing* is 'looseness of statement.'

let, v. 256, 'hinder'; A.S. *lettan*, 'to hinder,' literally 'to make *late*.' Cf. *Romans* i. 13, "oftentimes I purposed to come unto you, but was let hitherto," i.e. prevented.

lullaby, v. 48; an imitative word (see p. 140), formed from *lu lu* hummed by nurses in composing children to sleep.

madonna, 'my lady, madam'; the Fool's way of addressing Olivia; used only in this play. Ital. *ma*, 'my' + *donna*, 'lady' (Lat. *domina*).

malignancy, II. 1. 4. Used here, as *malignant* often is by Elizabethans, with reference to astrology. Cf. 1 *Henry VI*, IV. 5. 6, "O malignant and ill-boding stars." Lat. *malignus*, 'unkind, ill-disposed.' Astrology has stamped its mark on the language in such words as 'dis*aster*' (Lat. *astrum*, 'a star'), 'ill-*starred*,' 'jovial,' 'saturnine.'

marry; corrupted from the name of the 'Virgin *Mary*'; cf. "by'r *lady*" = 'by our Lady,' i.e. the Virgin. Such expressions dated from the pre-Reformation times in England. The common meanings of *marry* are 'indeed, to be sure' and 'why' (as an expletive implying some contempt). Sometimes joined with *amen* to affirm a wish or imprecation; cf. IV. 2. 109, and *Henry VIII*, III. 2. 54, "*Surrey:* The Lord forbid! *Norfolk:* Marry, amen!"

masque, or **mask,** I. 3. 121, 'an entertainment in which the performers wore *masks* or vizards.' From Arabic *maskharat*, 'a buffoon, jester, a pleasantry.' When *Twelfth Night* was written and up to about 1640 *masques* were very popular in England. They were a kind of private theatricals (with music) patronised by the Court and great nobles and Legal Societies (see p. x). There is a *masque* in *The Tempest*. A famous one is Milton's *Comus*.

minion, v. 128, 'favourite, darling'; F. *mignon*. Often contemptuous; cf. 3 *Henry VI*, II. 2. 84, "Go, rate thy minions, proud insulting boy!"

misprision, I. 5. 61, 'mistake, error'; cf. *Much Ado*, IV. 1. 187, "There is some strange misprision in the princes." O.F. *mesprision*, 'error,' from *mesprendre* (modern *méprendre*), 'to take amiss.' *Misprision* = 'contempt' is a separate word (from F. *priser*, 'to prize').

motley, I. 5. 63; properly (1) the fool's dress; sometimes (2) the fool himself, as in *Sonnet* 110, "made myself a motley." Also (3) used as adjective; cf. *Henry VIII*, Prologue 16, "a motley coat."

nayword, II. 3. 146, 'byword.' Used = 'watchword' in *The Merry Wives of Windsor*, II. 2. 131 and V. 2. 5. Said to belong to Warwickshire and the adjacent counties, like most of Shakespeare's dialect words; see *Shakespeare's England* (1916), II. 571–573.

needs, III. 2. 3, 'of necessity.' The genitive case of *need* and a survival of the old adverbial use of the genitive; cf. *willes*, 'willingly.'

nonpareil, I. 5. 273, 'a person unequalled, peerless'; cf. *Macbeth*, III. 4. 17, 19, "Thou art the best...Thou art the *nonpareil*." F. *non*, 'not' +*pareil*, 'equal'; cf. Lat. *par*, 'equal.'

numbers, II. 5. 111, 'metre'; more frequently='verse, poetry' (Lat. *numeri*). Cf. Pope, "I lisp'd in numbers, for the numbers came." So *numerous*='melodious' (Lat. *numerosus*); cf. *Paradise Lost*, V. 150, "in prose or numerous verse."

nuncio, I. 4. 28, 'messenger'; an Italian form from Lat. *nuncius*. Cf. Henry More (1640), "*Lucifer* laughs, bright Nuncio of the Day." Commonly *nuncio*=an ambassador or diplomatic envoy of the Pope.

orchard, III. 2. 8='garden.' This was the original sense, *orchard* being=*wort-yard*, 'herb-garden': *wort*='herb, plant.' Cf. Marlowe's *Hero and Leander*, II. 288, "Leander now... Enter'd the orchard of th' Hesperides," i.e. the 'garden.' *Garden* and *yard* are cognate.

othergates, V. 198; properly a genitive='of or in another gate,' i.e. 'way, manner,' the old sense of *gate*. Cf. Middle English *anothergates*, 'in another way, manner,' *thusgates*, 'in this way.'

owe, II. 4. 106, 108; properly 'to have, possess,' and so 'to bear towards, feel for.' Cf. *Venus and Adonis*, 523, "if any *love* you *owe* me." For *owe* in its original sense 'to possess' cf. *Macbeth*, I. 4. 10, "To throw away the dearest thing he owed." Akin to *own*.

pavin, V. 207; more often *pavan*, from F. *pavane*. A grave, dignified dance, of either Spanish or Italian origin; often mentioned by Elizabethans. Probably *pavan*=Low Lat. *pavanus*, 'like a peacock' (*pavo*), the dancers moving in a slow, stately manner (Skeat).

The particular kind of *pavan* alluded to in V. 207 was an Italian dance called the **passamezzo**, older form **passemezzo**, "an abbreviation of *passo e mezzo*, i.e. a step and a half, which may have formed a distinctive feature of the dance" (Grove's *Dict. of Music*). The Italian name naturally got corrupted in English, and some forms found in Elizabethan works, e.g. "Passa Measures Pavin," "Passmezures Pavan," differ little from Sir Toby's "passy measures." No doubt, *mezzo* was corrupted (by 'popular etymology') into *measures* through the use of *measure*='a stately dance'—cf. the phrase 'to tread a measure.'

For detailed accounts of the dances mentioned in this play see *Shakespeare's England* (1916), "Dancing."

peevish, I. 5. 319; 'childish,' 'silly,' 'perverse,' 'wayward.' Originally 'making a plaintive cry,' like the *peewit*.

point-devise, or **point-device**, II. 5. 176, 'exactly, precisely.' An adjective ='too precise, needlessly exact,' in *As You Like It*, III. 2. 401, "you are rather point-devise in your accoutrements"; and *Love's Labour's Lost*, V. 1. 21. Short for the old phrase *at point device* ='with great exactitude,' from O.F. *à point devis* =literally 'according to a point devised,' i.e. very precisely.

prank, II. 4. 89, 'to deck, adorn'; cf. *Winter's Tale*, IV. 4. 10, "most goddess-like pranked up"; Milton, *Comus*, 759, "false rules pranked in reason's garb." Akin to *prance* and Germ. *prunk*, 'pomp.'

prevent, III. 1. 94, 'anticipate, forestall'; cf. *Psalm* cxix. 148, "Mine eyes prevent the night watches," and I *Thessalonians* iv. 15, "we which are alive...shall not prevent them which are asleep," i.e. 'rise before.' Lat. *praevenire*, 'to come before.'

proper, II. 2. 30, III. 1. 144, 'handsome, fine, comely'; a common Elizabethan use. Portia describes her English suitor as "a proper man's picture," i.e. the very picture of a handsome man. In *Hebrews* xi. 23, "Moses...was hid three months of his parents, because they saw he was a proper child," the Revised Version substitutes 'goodly.'

quirk, III. 4. 268, 'humour'; cf. *All's Well That Ends Well*, III. 2. 51, "I have *felt* so many *quirks* of joy and grief." But commonly *quirk* implies something not felt but said—'a jest,' especially 'a stupid joke.' Cf. *Much Ado*, II. 3. 245, "odd quirks and remnants of wit."

renegado, III. 2. 74, 'an apostate, deserter'; =Spanish *renegado*, 'one who has denied the faith' (from Lat. *negare*, 'to deny'). Cf. Hakluyt's *Voyages* (1599), "a Spaniard renegado from the host." *Runagate* in *Psalm* lxviii. 6 (*Prayer-Book*) is a corruption of the word—"letteth the runagates continue in scarceness."

revels, I. 3 121; the special term for the Twelfth Night and similar festivities of the Legal Societies; cf. the definition of it in Minsheu's *Dictionary* (1617): "Sports of dauncing, *masking*, *comedies*, tragedies, and such like, used in the King's house, *the houses of Court*" (i.e. Inns of Court or Legal Societies). *Twelfth Night* itself formed part of the Middle Temple *revels* in Feb. 1602; see *Introduction*, p. x.

rule, II. 3. 132; commonly interpreted 'behaviour'; but *rule* was somewhat confused with *revel* from the similarity of their forms in Middle E., and there are passages in Elizabethan writers where *rule* seems to have the sense 'revel.' Perhaps *rule* ='revel' here, and "*night-rule*" ='night-revel,' in *Midsummer-Night's Dream*, III. 2. 5.

sack, II. 3. 206; formerly also written *seck*; a general name for the light *dry* wines imported from Spain and the Canary Isles, e.g. 'Sherris-*sack*' (as *sherry* was often called) and 'Canary-*sack*.' From Spanish *seco*, 'dry'; cf. the French *vin sec*.

sad, III. 4. 5, 21, 'grave, serious,' without any notion of sorrow; a common use then. Cf. *Henry V*, IV. 1. 318, "the sad and solemn priests"; and Milton, *Paradise Lost*, VI. 541, "in his face I see sad resolution." The original sense was 'sated,' A.S. *sæd* being akin to Lat. *satis*, 'enough.'

save, III. 1. 172, 'except'; *save* followed by the nominative case was a common idiom from Chaucer's time to Milton's. Cf. 1 *Kings* iii. 18, "there was no stranger with us in the house, save we two." So in *Paradise Lost*, II. 814, "*Save he* who reigns above, none can resist." In these instances *save* is a conjunction of participial origin, not a preposition, and probably came from an absolute construction. Thus "save I" may be short for 'I being save*d*' ='excepted.'

saw, III. 4. 413, 'a maxim, proverb'; A.S. *sagu*, 'a saying.' Cf. 2 *Henry VI*, I. 3. 61, "holy saws of sacred writ"; and *As You Like It*, II. 7. 156, "full of wise saws" (said of a judge).

shent, IV. 2. 112, 'rebuked, scolded'; cf. *Coriolanus*, V. 2. 104, "Do you hear how we are shent?" Shakespeare uses only the p. p. of *shend* which Spenser has often, especially ='to disgrace, shame'; cf. *The Faerie Queene*, IV. 1. 51.

skills, V. 295, 'matters, makes a difference'; cf. 2 *Henry VI*, III. 1. 281, "It skills not greatly who impugns our doom." From an Icelandic root ='to cleave, separate,' whence the metaphor 'to distinguish,' i.e. make a *difference* between things.

sonnet, III. 4. 25; now limited to a particular kind of poem of fourteen lines, but applied by Elizabethans to any kind of short poem or song, especially to love-poems. The poem to which Malvolio refers as a "sonnet" was really a ballad.

sooth, II. 4. 47, 'truth'; cf. *forsooth, soothsayer*. Used adverbially (II. 1. 11, II. 4. 91), *sooth* ='in sooth.' Adverbial phrases, from constant, colloquial use, have a tendency to abbreviate.

Sophy, II. 5. 198, III. 4. 307, 'the Shah of Persia'; cf. *Merchant of Venice*, II. 1. 25, "That slew the Sophy and a Persian prince." So in Ben Jonson's *Volpone* (1605), III. 5, "the Persian Sophy's wife." The word *Sophy* is a corruption of Arabic *safî*, 'elect,' 'chosen'; and *safî* was a title (like the 'Cæsar' of the Roman emperors) borne by each Shah or sovereign of the dynasty founded by Ismael which ruled Persia 1505–1725. The derivation of *Sophy* from *sūfī*, 'wise,' is wrong.

stuck, III. 4. 303, 'thrust in fencing'=Ital. *stoccata*; cf. *Hamlet*, IV. 7. 162, "your venomed stuck." Also called *stock*, *stoccado* and *stoccata*. Cf. Florio (1598), "a *thrust* or *stoccado*," and Jonson, *Every Man in his Humour*, I. 5, "you shall kill him... the first *stoccata*."

taffeta, II. 4. 77, 'fine, smooth silk stuff'; a favourite material of the Elizabethans. F. *taffetas* from Persian *táftah*, 'twisted, woven.'

tall, I. 3. 20, 'stout, valiant'; a colloquial use and generally ironical, as when Falstaff called Pistol and Nym "good soldiers and tall fellows," *Merry Wives of Windsor*, II. 2. 11.

testril, II. 3. 34, 'a sixpence'; first coined in the reign of Henry VIII, and then worth about a shilling. Also written *tester*, whence *tizzie*. Cf. 2 *Henry IV*, III. 2. 296, "there's a tester for thee." The *tester* was called after the French coin *testoon*, so named from the head (O.F. *teste*, F. *tête*) stamped upon it of Louis XII.

tilly-vally, II. 3. 83; an exclamation expressing contempt of something just said. Cf. Roper's *Life of Sir Thomas More*, "To whom shee,...not likeing such talke, answeared, '*Tille valle*, *Tille valle*'" (Pitt Press *Utopia*, p. xlv). Cf. too, Scott, *The Antiquary*, VI: "I shall be disappointed, sir, if I do not find the ladies very undeserving of your satire"..."Tilley-valley, Mr Lovel, Tilley-valley, I say—a truce with your politeness."

toy, III. 3. 44, V. 400, 'a trifle.' Cf. 2 *Henry IV*, II. 4. 183, "Shall we fall foul for toys?" i.e. quarrel about trifles. Akin to Germ. *zeug*, 'stuff, trash'; e.g. in *spielzeug*, 'playthings.'

tuck, III. 4. 244, 'rapier'; a corruption through F. *estoc* of Ital. *stocco*, 'a short sword.'

unhatched, III. 4. 257; commonly taken =*unhacked*, i.e. not cut or dinted by blows given and received in battle. *Hatch* = F. *hacher*, which Cotgrave explains "to *hacke*, slice." "Cross-*hatching*" is an engraver's term.

viol-de-gamboys, I. 3. 27, a corruption of Ital. *viola da gamba*, 'the bass viol'; so called because held between the legs of the player (Ital. *gamba*='leg,' F. *jambe*). The viol, of which there were four kinds, was the forerunner of the violin and in use up to the last century. The violin (invented in Italy about 1650) gradually, on account of its louder tone, displaced the Treble, Tenor and Bass viols, only the Double Bass or violone surviving. In Shakespeare's time the viol was a favourite instrument. The Italian name *viola da gamba* was partly Anglicised then as *viol de gambo*; cf. the title of Douland's "First Booke of Songes or Ayres...sung to the Lute, Orpherian or *Viol de* *gambo*" (1597). Hence Sir Toby's pronunciation was not far removed from the current form.

weed, v. 262, 280, 'dress'; A.S. *wæd*, 'garment.' Cf. *Coriolanus*, II. 3. 161, "With a proud heart he wore his humble weeds." Now limited to the phrase 'widow's weeds,' except in poetry; cf. Tennyson, "In words like weeds I'll wrap me o'er" (*In Memoriam*, v.).

welkin, II. 3. 59, 'sky'; properly a plural word ='clouds,' from A.S. *wolcnu*, the plural of *wolcen*, 'a cloud'; cf. the cognate Germ. *wolke*, 'a cloud.'

westward-ho, III. 1. 145; "to the west: an old cry of London watermen on the Thames in hailing passengers bound westward" (i.e. up the river). The opposite cry, of course, was "eastward-ho!"=down the Thames to places like Deptford, Greenwich, etc.

wreck, v. 82; in the 1st Folio always spelt *wrack*, the usual form till late in the 17th century, cf. the rhyme in *Macbeth*, v. 5. 51:

> "Blow, wind! come, *wrack*!
> At least we'll die with harness on our *back*."

In "*rack* and ruin" we should write *wrack*. A.S. *wrecan*, 'to drive,' the *wrack* or *wreck*=what is driven ashore.

yare, III. 4. 244, 'sharp, nimble, ready'; cf. *Measure for Measure*, IV. 2. 61, "if you have occasion to use me, you shall find me yare." Often an adverb; cf. *The Tempest*, I. 1. 7, "yare, yare! Take in the topsail." A.S. *gearu*, 'ready'; *g* frequently softens into *y*.

yeoman, II. 5. 45, 'servant,' its meaning in Chaucer; cf. *The Prologue* to the *Canterbury Tales*, 101, "A *yeman* hadde he, and *servaunts* na-mo." So in 2 *Henry IV*, II. 1. 4, *yeoman* means 'attendant' (viz. upon a sheriff or bailiff). Its usual sense in Elizabethan writers, as now, is 'farmer, small freeholder,' the first part of the word probably signifying 'village' or 'country, district.' "*Yeoman's* service" (*Hamlet*, v. 2. 36) was "good, loyal service such as a *yeoman* or freeholder performed for his feudal lord."

zanies, I. 5. 96. The *zany* was a stock-character of Italian comedies, being a subordinate buffoon who had to imitate clumsily the tricks and humours of the chief clown; cf. Ben Jonson, *Cynthia's Revels*, II. 1, "The other gallant is his *zany*... sweats [i.e. labours] to *imitate* him in everything." *Zany*=Ital. *zanni*, a corruption of *Giovanni*, 'John,' Gk 'Ιωάννης; cf. the slang term 'a Johnny.'

APPENDIX

SHAKESPEARE AND PURITANISM

Twelfth Night is commonly thought to contain some indication of Shakespeare's feelings towards Puritanism. The word "Puritan" occurs three times in the play (II. 3. 152, 155, 159). It is applied to Malvolio—as "*sometimes a kind*[1] of Puritan."

To attempt to infer Shakespeare's own opinions from his plays is hazardous. What a dramatist makes his characters say may not be at all what he himself, speaking in his own person, would say. But we may fairly suppose that had Shakespeare been in sympathy with Puritanism the term "Puritan" would not have been used of a character who is covered with ridicule as Malvolio is; and we must remember that it occurs elsewhere, e.g. in *All's Well That Ends Well*, I. 3. 56, 98, in a contemptuous context. It is safe, I think, to credit Shakespeare with some dislike of Puritanism and to regard the passages in *Twelfth Night* and *All's Well* as casual expressions of that dislike. The causes of his feeling are not far to seek.

In the first place, there was a bitter, long-standing feud between the play-writers (and play-goers) and the Puritans. Puritanism had opposed the theatre in every way and tried hard to suppress it altogether. The dramatists naturally retorted by heaping ridicule upon their enemy. "Gibes, taunts, caricatures in ridicule and aspersion of Puritans and Puritanism make up a great part of the comic literature of the later Elizabethan drama."

As an actor therefore and play-writer Shakespeare might be expected to cherish and express a feeling of hostility to the Puritans.

Again, Puritanism, with all its sterling qualities, had a certain narrowness and intolerance altogether alien to the broad and tolerant impartiality of Shakespeare. He identified himself with no party or sect. He represented the full enlightenment of his age, and more. What most distinguishes him when he deals with religious matters is his absolute freedom from bias. "He was no fanatic and no infidel, no atheist and no mystic, no Brownist and no politician." He preserved always a "wonderful medium between narrow-mindedness and extreme," and dealt

---

[1] Part of the taunt therefore is that Malvolio is not a consistent, honest Puritan.

fairly with all forms of religious conviction. To a man of such
tolerance the intolerance of the Puritan spirit cannot have been
congenial.

But while recognising that Shakespeare's personal dislike of
the Puritans finds vent, to a certain extent, in *Twelfth Night*, I
do not think that we are justified in regarding his delineation
of the character of Malvolio as a " grand attack upon them."
Hunter, who adopts this view in his well-known paper on the
subject, says: " there is a systematic design of holding them [the
Puritans] up to ridicule, and of exposing to public odium what
appeared to him to be the dark features in the Puritan character.
...Shakespeare intended to make Malvolio an abstract of that
character, to exhibit in him all the worst features....His object
was to hold up the Puritan to aversion....In Malvolio's general
character the intention was to make the Puritan odious."

Surely this overstates the case—reads into the play something
more than is really there. Sustained and bitter satire would be
out of place in a piece so light and bright as *Twelfth Night*. Its
tone is good humour. Malvolio is made ridiculous but scarcely
"odious." One does not think of " dark features " in his character. There is, I hope, pity as well as "aversion" in our laughter
at him: Olivia at any rate is sorry for him. We must not take
Malvolio's faults too seriously or too harshly.

If Shakespeare had deliberately set to work to satirise Puritanism and make it appear contemptible he would have painted the
picture in deeper colours. But I do not believe that he had any
such design, or that these allusions in the play are anything but
passing strokes of sarcasm which just indicate—and no more—
his attitude of unfriendliness towards the Puritan movement.
On the general relation of the Puritans towards the stage see
some remarks in *Kenilworth*, xvii. (Pitt Press ed. p. 250), a novel
full of Shakespearian allusions and words which add greatly to
the Elizabethan colouring. See also *Shakespeare's England*, I.
57-59.

HINTS ON SHAKESPEARE'S ENGLISH

THE following elementary hints are intended to remind young students of some simple but important facts which they are apt to forget when asked to explain points of grammar and idiom in Shakespeare's English.

To begin with, avoid using the word "mistake" in connection with Shakespearian English. Do not speak of "Shakespeare's mistakes." In most cases the "mistake" will be yours, not his. Remember that things in his English which appear to us irregular may for the most part be explained by one of two principles:

(1) The difference between Elizabethan and modern English;
(2) The difference between spoken and written English.

(1) As to the former: what is considered bad English now may have been considered good English in Shakespeare's time. Language must change in the space of 300 years. Elizabethan English, recollect, contains an element of Old English, i.e. inflected English that had case-endings for the nouns, terminations for the verbs, and the like. By the end of the 16th century most of these inflections had died out, but some survived, and the influence of the earlier inflected stage still affected the language. Often when we enquire into the history of some Elizabethan idiom which seems to us curious we find that it is a relic of an old usage. Let us take an example.

There are numerous cases in Shakespeare where a verb in the present tense has the inflection -s, though the subject is plural; cf. the following lines in *Richard II*, II. 3. 4, 5:

> "These high wild hills and rough uneven ways
> *Draws* out our miles, and *makes* them wearisome."

The verbs *draws* and *makes* appear to be singular; but probably each is plural, in agreement with its plural antecedents *hills* and *ways*; *s = es* being the plural inflection of the present tense used in the Northern dialect of old English. In the Southern dialect the inflection was *eth*; in the Midland *en*. When Shakespeare was born all three forms were getting obsolete; but all three are found in his works, *eth*[1] and *en*[2] very rarely, *es* or *s* many times.

---

[1] Cf. *hath* and *doth* used as plurals.
[2] Cf. *wax-en* in *Midsummer-Night's Dream*, II. 1. 56; see *G.* to that play.

His use of the last is a good illustration (a) of the difference[1] between Shakespearian and modern English, (b) of one of the main causes of that difference—viz. the influence of a still earlier inflected English.

(2) A dramatist makes his characters speak, and tells his story through their mouths: he is not like a historian who writes the story in his own words. The English of a play which is meant to be spoken must not be judged by the same standard as the English of a History which is meant to be read. For consider how much more correct and regular in style a book usually is than a speech or a conversation. In speaking we begin a sentence one way and we may finish it in another, some fresh idea striking us or some interruption occurring. Speech is liable to constant changes, swift turns of thought; it leaves things out, supplying the omission, very likely, with a gesture; it often combines two forms of expression. But a writer can correct and polish his composition until all irregularities are removed. Spoken English therefore is less regular[2] than written English; and it is to this very irregularity that Shakespeare's plays owe something of their lifelike reality. If Shakespeare made his characters speak with the correctness of a copybook we should regard them as mere puppets, not as living beings.

Here is a passage taken from *Henry V* (IV. 3. 34–36); suppose that comment on its "grammatical peculiarities" is required:

> "Rather proclaim it...
> That he which hath no stomach to this fight,
> Let him depart."

Two things strike us at once—"he *which*" and "That he...let him depart." "He *which*" is now bad English; then it was quite regular English. The student should say that the usage was correct in Elizabethan English, and give some illustration of it. The Prayer-Book will supply him with a very familiar one.

"That he...let him depart." A prose-writer would have finished with the regular sequence "*may* depart." But Henry V is supposed to say the words; and at the moment he is deeply stirred. Emotion leads him to pass suddenly from indirect to direct speech. The conclusion, though less regular, is far more vivid. This brief passage therefore exemplifies the difference (a) between Elizabethan English and our own, (b) between

---

[1] Another aspect of it is the free Elizabethan use of participial and adjectival terminations. Cf. "estimable," II. I. 28; "incredulous," III. 4. 88; "deceivable," IV. 3. 21.

[2] Note the irregular sequence of tenses in Shakespeare; cf. III. 2. 65.

spoken English and written. It is useful always to consider whether the one principle or the other can be applied.

Three general features of Elizabethan English should be observed:

(1) its brevity,
(2) its emphasis,
(3) its tendency to interchange parts of speech.

(1) *Brevity*. Shakespeare often uses terse elliptical turns of expression. The following couplet is from *Troilus and Cressida* (1. 3. 287, 288):

"And may that soldier a mere recreant prove
That means not, hath not, or is not in love!"

Put fully, the second line would run, "That means not *to be*, hath not *been*, or is not in love." Cf. again *Richard II*, v. 5. 26, 27:

"Who sitting in the stocks refuge their shame,
That many have and others must sit there";

i.e. 'console themselves with the thought that many have *sat* there.' This compactness of diction is very characteristic of Shakespeare. For note that the omission of the italicised words, while it shortens the form of expression, does not obscure the sense, since the words are easily supplied from the context. That is commonly the case with Shakespeare's *ellipses* or omissions: they combine brevity with clearness. See 1. 1. 34, 11. 4. 99, 111. 3. 40, v. 37, 89; and for omission of the relative pronoun, a frequent and important *ellipse*, cf. 1. 5. 108, 123, 11. 4. 89, 110 (with the *Notes*).

(2) *Emphasis*. Common examples of this are the double negative (11. 1. 1, IV. 1. 6), and the double comparative or superlative; cf. *The Tempest*, 1. 2. 19, 20, "I am more better than Prospero," and *Julius Cæsar*, III. 1. 121, "With the most boldest and best hearts of Rome."

(3) *Parts of speech interchanged*. "Almost any part of speech can be used as any other part of speech" (Abbott). Cf. 1. 5. 141, 11. 3. 145, 111. 2. 48, 111. 3. 24, 111. 4. 82, 100, 222, 253, IV. 2. 99, v. 1. 86, and see the *Notes* on these passages.

Two or three other points in *Twelfth Night* may be classified under "grammar" and noted here.

1. 2. 35: *What's she?* What sort of person? A common phrase in Shakespeare. It is not that *what* is put for *who*, but that the speaker enquires as to the rank or condition of the person. A natural first question to ask in times "when the distinction between ranks was much more marked than now"—Abbott.

v. 1. 123: *But hear me this*; literally 'for me' (the indirect object); but this so-called "ethic" dative often has an emphasising force = 'mark you,' 'just,' 'please to.' So here it is like some gesture of emphasis. See III. 2. 35 (note). In I. 2. 53, "conceal me what I am," some take *me* as an ethic dative (= 'for me, in my interest'); perhaps, rightly.

v. 1. 135: *most jocund, apt and willingly*. The adverbial suffix must go with *apt*, and probably qualifies *jocund* also. Shakespeare often makes one termination serve for a pair of words in close relation, and sometimes extends the licence to three words. Cf. *The Comedy of Errors*, v. 88, "When he demean'd himself rough, rude and wildly"; *Sonnet* 80, "The humble as the proudest sail"; *Cymbeline*, IV. 2. 347, "I fast and prayed for their intelligence, thus."

INDEX OF WORDS, PHRASES AND NAMES

This list applies to the NOTES *only; words of which longer explanations are given will be found in the* GLOSSARY. *The references are to the pages.*

ABBREVIATIONS:

adj. = adjective   adv. = adverb   n. = noun   vb = verb

CAMBRIDGE: PRINTED BY W. LEWIS. M.A., AT THE UNIVERSITY PRESS